Praise for Ellen B

"I found myself excited in a Tony Robbins sort of way taw boundaries and regain control of the parts of my life that ha. On the surface, this book may appear like that of a traditional caregiver book. But Ellen Besso is a life coach, and the words "victim" and "cannot" are not words commonly used by coaches. It's here where Besso's book creates separation and a credibility that cannot be denied."
Ryan Malone, author of *Inside Elder Care* - http://www.insideeldercare.com

"Walk with Ellen Besso as she helps you explore and understand the intricacies of caregiving. Let her teach you how to set boundaries, ask for help, release guilt, and make caring for self a priority. Everyone will benefit. "
Dotsie Bregel, Founder, National Association of Baby Boomer Women
http://www.NABBW.com http://www.BoomerWomenSpeak.com

"Ellen Besso is an amazing life coach who helps women navigate through the incredible journey of midlife. She is also a personal friend that I've known for the past 4 years. We bonded during our life coaching training with Oprah Magazine columnist and world famous life coach Martha Beck. Ellen has written an incredibly insightful book entitled *Surviving Eldercare: Where Their Needs End and Yours Begin* that helps women successfully navigate the stages of caring for an elderly parent. I'm confident you will find the book a must read for anyone caring for an elderly parent while trying to live as normal a life as possible. Job well done Ellen! "
Sheryl Jones, R U Happe Life Coaching - http://ruhappe.com

"What a terrific book! Even though my 25+ years of caregiving have recently come to an end, *Surviving Eldercare: Where Their Needs End and Yours Begin* helped me so much to put my eldercare stage of life into perspective and look forward to the next phase. Ellen's book is a must-read for any caregiver – past, present, or future. "
Barbara E. Friesner, creator of The Ultimate Caregiver's Success System
http://www.AgeWiseLiving.com

"Excellent eldercare survival guide! Ellen has an amazing gift for helping us thrive while caring for our elders and coping with the challenges of midlife, because in addition to a Masters in Counseling Psychology and being a Registered Clinical Counselor, she's been a devoted caregiver to her mother who suffers from Alzheimer's - for more than a decade! "
Jacqueline Marcell, author of *Elder Rage* and host of *Coping with Caregiving* radio show

Surviving Eldercare:

Where Their Needs End

and Yours Begin

Book I of the *MidLife Balance* series

by Ellen Besso

First Edition published March, 2009
Second Edition published May, 2009
Print Edition published September 2009

All rights reserved.

No part of this book may be reproduced in any form or by an electronic or mechanical means including information storage and retrieval systems without permission in writing from the author, except by a reviewer who may quote brief passages in a review.

The suggestions put forward in this publication and the accompanying exercise booklet are not meant to take the place of professional advice, therapy or services.

The author disclaims any liability arising directly or indirectly from the use of this book.

Printed and bound in Canada by Printorium Bookworks
A Division of Island Blue Print Co. Ltd., Victoria, BC
www.islandblue.com

ISBN: 978-0-9812381-0-4

Ellen Besso
800 961 1364 (North America Toll-Free)
604 886 1916 (Sunshine Coast)
info@ellenbesso.com

Table of Contents

INTRODUCTION 1

CHAPTER 1 - WHO ARE YOU? 5

CHAPTER 2 - TRYING TO DO TOO MUCH 11

CHAPTER 3 - HOW WE CHANGE IN MIDLIFE 17

CHAPTER 4 – HOW OUR RELATIONSHIPS CHANGE 23

CHAPTER 5 - THOUGHTS THAT RUN THE SHOW 31

CHAPTER 6 - TAKING CARE OF YOU 35

CHAPTER 7 - DEALING WITH MANY EMOTIONS AS A CAREGIVER 41

CHAPTER 8 - ASKING FOR HELP 47

CHAPTER 9 - YOUR SPIRITUAL CONNECTION 53

CHAPTER 10 - PUTTING IT ALL TOGETHER 57

A NEW WAY OF LIVING 61

EXERCISE BOOKLET 63

Introduction

Putting ourselves first is a concept that is very difficult for women to hear. It goes against the grain. After all, we're women, aren't we meant to nurture? Years ago when I was in group therapy, the facilitator used to tell us to put ourselves first. As many of us were mothers, that made her request an especially tough one.

It took many attempts on the part of the therapist before we began to understand what she was talking about. What finally convinced us was the idea that we would be better mothers, partners, workers - as well as better human beings - if we prioritized our own needs.

Maybe I've been one of the lucky ones. I didn't buy into the 'relentless busyness' of modern life, as Wayne Muller, author of *Sabbath: Restoring the Sacred Rhythm of Rest and Delight*, calls it. This may have been partly due to my increased awareness from being in the group, my partner's balanced way of living and also the result of the deliberate choices we made together about the lifestyle we wanted and where we chose to live.

Although city people, in the eighties we made our home in an old farmhouse just north of Toronto, and since 1990 we've called a BC coastal community a forty-minute ferry ride from Vancouver our home. Even when we went back to city living for almost five years early in this decade, serendipity provided us with a slower-paced living situation in a very special little community called *Quayside Village Co-housing*. Life within the community is a microcosm of a slower society, where neighbours stop to pass the time of day, have tea together and share common meals twice each week.

When Oprah Winfrey first had life coach Cheryl Richardson on her show in the early nineties, the audience actually booed her when she advised them to put themselves first, a surprising and unusual reaction on their part. They obviously felt very strongly about this topic, perhaps because of their conditioning combined with their biology of nurturing hormones.

Certainly things have changed since then, but I'm not sure just how much. Many women now take the advice of professionals and carve out some regular time for themselves. They may have a massage now and then or take an hour alone or with friends. However, to ensure our needs are fully met, we need to carefully develop a daily rhythm of mindful balance. It's our right and we're entitled to this.

The responsibility of caregiving is still considered women's work almost exclusively in our society. Most paid and unpaid caregivers are female. Our elders rely on their daughters, daughters-in-law and granddaughters for help if they do not have a spouse to care for them.

Introduction

Many of us have been raised to believe our job is to take care of our family's needs, including those of our aging parents. This is particularly true of women born in the babyboomer years (1946 to 1965).

For the past ten years I have been a caregiver for my mother who has Alzheimer's Disease. I haven't done it solo, my brother took a very active role in the first years, organizing and managing her in-home care as well as visiting our mom regularly. We've been very fortunate to have many loving private and care home professionals who have done most of the practical work of looking after mom.

The midlife caregiver experience can be very stressful. Midlife is a time when our focus and our energies are shifting inward, yet now we have an additional responsibility. It's easy to lose sight of ourselves during the process of taking care of aging parents. This can be especially true in a shared living situation, where the caregiver is available to her parent around the clock.

It may be some time before we begin to realize, and even longer before we acknowledge, that a large part of the stress we're experiencing with its accompanying sadness, guilt and frustration, is a result of our complicated relationship with our declining parent. At first we may think it's our job, our business, our partner or our kids that are the cause of our nagging worries.

When we do become aware of the root of our problem, we often feel we shouldn't complain. After all they're our parents and we have a duty to them. Perhaps we say to ourselves, "What right do I have to feel burdened when I'm not doing the bulk of the daily care?"

Finding the balance between the doing and the being - between the demands of the outer, physical world and our inner emotional and spiritual one - is so important for women. There are many reasons midlife might not be the ideal time for caregiving. We may yearn to begin new ventures such as travel, school, volunteer work, hobbies or a new business, our energy levels may be lower, we may be experiencing health issues including perimenopause and menopause challenges, or we may want to retire and do whatever pleases us.

Humans are like plants. It takes a lot to kill most plants. They can survive for years in poor soil, and poor light. But it's not good enough for us to just survive…to 'get through' our parent's declining years. We deserve much more than that. If we burn ourselves out it's difficult to recover a state of good health and joyful living.

For the most part no one is able to put herself first at all times. We deserve to experience life as full human beings… multi-faceted women. Only by feeding ourselves in every way possible will we be empowered to live the rich and joyful lives we yearn for and deserve.

No one would dispute that it's a challenge to live mindfully when we have demanding lives with many responsibilities. There is no easy answer for how to do this. This book will help by stimulating you to think *'outside the box'*. It will also provide exercises and worksheets for making the changes you desire in your life. Please do the exercises. They are designed to help you get a fresh perspective on yourself, your life and your needs, and to provide concrete, workable plans.

This is not a book of practical *'how-to's'*, although you will find some useful tips in it. There are many helpful books like that available. This is a book about change. It's about digging a little deeper into yourself… questioning… asking yourself if you are happy with the choices you're making in your life… if you're doing what you love to do. You may be familiar with some of the ideas mentioned, but good things bear repeating. We've all heard that we need to hear things many times before they really sink in.

My hope is that *Where Their Needs End and Yours Begin* will help you consider your physical, emotional, mental and spiritual needs in every aspect of your life… in the workplace, in relationships with others and most importantly, in your relationship with yourself.

I challenge you to question your beliefs and to change your thinking and your habits around being a midlife caregiver. It won't happen overnight. Change takes time, contrary to what the *'quick fix'* marketing tells us. When we are aware of our own needs, we can develop new ways of caring for those of our parent. Once we have created balance in our lives, we have the foundation to build our dreams on.

The Chapters

Each chapter of this book talks about a different aspect of our life as a *MidLife Caregiver*. There is a separate, complementary *Exercise Booklet* to help you consider your life as a woman and as a caregiver.

- ➢ Chapter 1, *Who Are You?*, profiles the wide range of women who make up the caregiver demographic.
- ➢ Chapter 2, *Trying To Do Too Much*, delves into many of the reasons we attempt to do so much as women.
- ➢ Chapter 3, *How We Change in MidLife*, discusses the subtle changes that happen in us as midlife women.
- ➢ Chapter 4, *How Our Relationships Change*, shows the impact our internal changes have on all our relationships, and on our willingness and ability to caregive.
- ➢ Chapter 5, *Thoughts That Run the Show*, outlines the major influence our thoughts and beliefs have on our lives as women.

- ➢ Chapter 6, *Taking Care of You*, covers the basics of caring for ourselves.
- ➢ Chapter 7, *Dealing With Many Emotions as a Caregiver*, addresses the interplay of our feelings as midlife women and our caregiver role.
- ➢ Chapter 8, *Asking For Help*, considers why we need help as caregivers and what often stops us from asking for it.
- ➢ Chapter 9, *Your Spiritual Connection*, suggests ways to personalize your spirituality and ways spirituality can bring comfort and renewal to caregivers.
- ➢ Chapter 10, *Putting It All Together*, summarizes the important aspects of midlife caregiving.

This book is meant to support you, the *Midlife Caregiver*, in your struggle to achieve balance in your life – the kind of balance that will ensure that you don't lose yourself in the lives of those you care for.

Ellen Besso, MidLife Coach & Writer

Chapter 1 - Who Are You?

Women are caregivers

- Do you worry your parent might be lonely or unsafe when you're not with them?
- Do you feel there must be more that you could be doing?
- Are you tired, stressed, resentful, guilty or physically unwell?
- Do you get frustrated and angry with other family members?
- Do you feel sad, powerless or fearful about your parent's declining condition?

If any of the above issues resonate with you, you have joined the growing ranks of midlife caregivers. The *MidLife Caregiver* could be any woman... she's the next door neighbor, the person in the next office, the woman in the grocery store, or maybe she's us. We often don't know the stories of other women's lives until we stop and talk with them, then we find we share many similarities. I am a life coach, a counselor and a mother and I am one of you. My brother Johnny and I have been responsible for our mother's well-being for the past ten years, ever since she asked us for help and opted to move to our community from Vancouver Island. During the first five years Johnny's role was that of self-appointed case manager, looking after many details of our mother's life, including hiring and supervising in-home care. His stress level increased over time as mom's Alzheimer's worsened, she became less safe and her needs more urgent. Sometimes there were phone calls to him late in the night.

Being a caregiver to my parent, who is frail physically and has severe dementia, is a much bigger responsibility than I expected it would be. For the past five years I've been the 'point woman' who oversees mom's care. I've provided hands-on care including personal hygiene, taken mom on weekly outings and to appointments, hosted occasional overnight visits, bought all her clothes and toiletries and paid her bills. Additionally, I've given her consistent emotional support and connection to a world that slowly, year by year, slips from her grasp.

Most adult women are already caregivers of some kind or other – for kids, family, friends or coworkers. Some of us have professional careers in caregiving also (such as nurses, care aides, counselors, teachers, doctors). Although gender roles are somewhat more flexible now, when it comes to caregiving our roles and responsibilities as women are very often still assumed. We don't feel we have much choice.

By midlife many of us are confronted with an additional caregiving responsibility – one that we may not have anticipated or given a lot of thought to previously. Only thirty-five to forty percent of women interviewed had considered and discussed the possibility of being a caregiver to their parent, according to a *Journal of Women & Aging* study done by Laditka & Pappas-Rogich.

The challenge of aging parents coincides with perimenopause, menopause and the beginning of new projects and transitions. We may still have adolescent or young adult children at home, or we're grandparents by now. The *'sandwich generation'* label that describes women squished between younger and older family members fits many of us.

The US Department of Health Womens' Services reports that female caregivers make up seventy-three percent of all caregivers. Our average age is around forty-six (I was forty-nine when I began caregiving for my mom). Caregiving seems to be *'women's work'* in a way that housework was in previous generations.

Men are socialized to assume fewer caring responsiblities throughout their life than women. Additionally some research suggests that males have a different view of caregiving than women in a couple of ways. The male approach emphasizes delegating responsibility and also recognizes that there are limitations to what one can accomplish. It seems a healthy philosophy to me, and perhaps women could benefit from these ideas.

Unpaid caregiving can take many forms

A daughter who shops for her aging parent, one who lives in another province or state and hires a private local care manager, a son who manages his parent's finances, a daughter-in-law who visits her parent in their care home and takes her on outings, or an adult child who lives with their parent all constitute caregivers. Long distance caregiving, sometimes called *'the geographic crunch'* or *'suitcase caregiving'*, is a worrisome job, and it is becoming more common as baby boomers and their parents age and live farther apart.

For two periods of time during the past ten years I've lived a forty-minute ferry ride plus a short drive from my mother. We were on opposite sides of the inlet between North Vancouver and the Sunshine Coast, British Columbia, waiting for a bed to become available for her in a care home during each of these periods. It took the better part of a day to visit her and take her on an outing.

As she deteriorated, I felt badly about leaving her at the door of her apartment, and later saying goodbye to her at her care home, although to a lesser extent. Even though my mother had others nearby, I was unsettled and worried about what might happen when I wasn't there, and about not being able to get to her if she had an accident or heart attack in the night when the ferries weren't running.

The reality of a caregiver's life

As most women are juggling caregiving around their paid work and their home life, they experience added stress. The unpaid caregiver often takes on enormous responsibility. The job of caregiving impacts all facets of our lives, from our time, to our finances, to the energy we have available for other activities and people.

Caregivers spend considerable time worrying or otherwise thinking about their parent. We wonder how they're managing when they're alone, how they're spending their time, and if they are safe. Research affirms my personal belief that the toll the emotional stress takes on caregivers is greater than that of the physical work.

The way we're affected depends on:
- The relationship we have with our parent.
- Our own emotional makeup.
- Our belief system about caregiving.

Adding to the stress is the sense many women have that other people do not understand the enormous amount of space the caregiving takes up in their life – *in our innermost self* - as well as in our schedule. Others may not have a living elderly parent or they may not feel the same desire to help their parent as we do. Claire Berman, author of *"Caring for Yourself While Caring for Your Aging Parents"*, said she felt consumed by her very elderly mother and mother-in-law's situations.

Despite the high level of responsibility we take on as caregivers, it's invisible work for the most part, because it's done in the home, and it's not officially sanctioned as a *'real job'* by our society and our government, hence there are no government benefits.

The demands of juggling caregiving around paid work and home life can feel overwhelming at times. Women in this position often don't realize the amount of work they are doing, what they're giving up personally. The pressure creeps up slowly over the years and we begin to notice it in our bodies, minds and emotions.

A number of caregivers develop stress-related health issues like high blood pressure and depression, and some are at high risk for heart disease. Sometimes we aren't sure how to quiet our anxiety and feelings of depression, so we turn to medication for help. The underlying reasons often remain unchanged.

Caregiving and our place in the workforce

Women, on average, earn less than men, and as we age our incomes fall further behind; caregiving often adds to our financial disadvantage as women.

It is difficult to perform well at work and as a caregiver; many women are forced to miss work, cut hours, quit their jobs or perhaps retire early to care for their elderly parent. This will ultimately affect their financial situation in later years.

Caregiving interferes more with our daily lives than men's caregiving duties do. Health Canada studies suggest that the greater emotional impact of caregiving on women is due firstly to the fact that caregiving is central to most women's identities, and secondly, because of the stressful nature of the intimate and emotional tasks they carry out. About a year ago when we began my mother's first proper dental care in twenty-five years, I found it emotionally challenging to support her during this process. But she's a real trouper and we all got through it!

Caregiver <u>and</u> daughter

Watching our once high-functioning parent deteriorate physically and sometimes mentally is a painful experience. Recently I sat with my mother on my back porch, watching and listening as she struggled unsuccessfully to put her thoughts into words. I affirmed that it must be a frustrating experience for her and she agreed. Other adult children are challenged by their parent's physical deterioration.

Our parents still hold power over us; most of us want to please our parent. Often there is a sense of obligation towards them that is mixed with love. Sometimes our desire to help ease their life is combined with resentment. This may lead to strong feelings of guilt.

Despite our willingness to help and our commitment to our parent, our internal resources begin to ebb after a few years, and we experience the symptoms of long term strain.

The impact of caregiving on me has been all-encompassing. Although I don't spend a great deal of time with her, my mother is in my conscious awareness often, and I'm quite certain she's always in my unconscious. This speaks to the idea of caregiving being central to the identity of women. It also relates to the family values I was brought up with, my personal belief system, and whatever unfinished business may remain between my mother and I.

I've been one of the fortunate ones, my brother has also been involved in my mother's care, and financial resources are available to provide whatever paid care is necessary. We were blessed with loving, competent in-home caregivers until our mother's quality of life was no longer viable at home, and after going into care mom has been content and very well looked after by the caring, loving professionals in two care facilities.

Yet it has been a trying time, and after ten years it's wearing. The five years as primary caregiver seem longer to me than the actual calendar time. It's easy to discount all I've done. Always there are the nagging thoughts: "Shouldn't I be doing more?", "Don't good daughters invite their mothers into their homes?", "Is it alright to fly to the other side of the world to travel and volunteer?".

As women, we expect a lot of ourselves. When it comes to caregiving, perhaps we set the toughest parameters of all. Consequently the pressure on us is great. But the good news is that there is much we can do to improve our situation. As we begin to look at the bigger picture of our lives, to identify what is important to us, and to take steps to meet our own needs, we will develop a positive, healthful way of living.

NOTES:

Chapter 2 - Trying to Do Too Much

You are undoubtedly a woman who is trying to do too much if:
- There aren't enough hours in the day to do what you need to do.
- Responsibilities feel too big for one woman to manage.
- You find it hard to say '*no*' to requests.
- Your personal life has faded into non-existence.
- You feel depleted, sad or resentful.

To many women it feels natural, even expected, to nurture others and help make their lives easier. I was brought up to please, and spent my earlier years functioning automatically for the most part, from my conditioning, with the unfortunate end result that I became a young woman who didn't really know who she was or what she wanted. Other women may have had different upbringings, but through a chain of circumstances, find themselves with unwieldy family and career responsibilities.

As women, we often enjoy connecting with others and are very good at supporting them. Some social scientists, like Carol Gilligan, believe that women are guided by '*an ethic of care*' that leads us to be concerned with personal relationships. Women often prefer to avoid conflict, so we may not articulate our own needs and desires.

When we can't give ourselves permission to seek what we want, we live our lives playing the roles of worker, mother, partner, daughter, community member and so on. Over time we may begin to think the needs of our partner, our children and our aging parents are actually our own needs, says Jean Baker Miller. We have *become* our roles rather than *performing* them.

Doing it all

We're great at multi-tasking and balancing many tasks with ease. We embody many roles and perform them with amazing efficiency. I remember how I prided myself on my great multi-tasking abilities in my twenties and thirties. In an office setting I could keep several balls in the air at once. As I grew older, I had a desire to focus more, so I chose a path that allowed me to concentrate on one task at a time rather than constantly moving from one to the other.

We have lives that are too busy for one person to handle with comfort. Sometimes we take on extra duties, perhaps filling in until someone is hired or recovers from an illness. Whatever the reason we just keep doing the extra work, being overwhelmed usually creeps up on us slowly over time, outside our awareness.

- If we take a close look at *what we're doing* and *why we're doing it* we can make some inroads towards reducing our schedules.
- Over-scheduling and multi-tasking will seldom be required when we pare our work down to a manageable level.

When the founder of the online community *Momasource* sent out a questionnaire to members, women's responses to the question "What intrinsic qualities do women have that give them a competitive edge over men?" exemplified their pride in their ability to multi-task and to manage over-scheduled lives.
- The majority of respondents touted their multi-tasking expertise by an overwhelming margin.
- Heather Lawrence of *Texas Stork* challenged men to: "Talk on the phone, send a fax, reply to an e-mail, change a diaper, get a toddler a snack, monitor school-age children's TV shows and add to the grocery list — all at the same time."[1]

What is this brilliance costing us? It seems that this adeptness, based on *perceived necessity* and perhaps on competitiveness, is a double-edged sword, turning on us when we're least expecting it, in the form of stress, anxiety, guilt and physical ailments.

When we hit midlife, the ability and often the desire to switch from one focus to another effortlessly and quickly begins to diminish. Some studies suggest multi-tasking skills decrease in midlife because they're *estrogen-facilitated*. This is good news. We can manage it if we must, but it is not our preferred way of functioning in the world. This gives us a chance to slow down, engage fully in each activity and then segue slowly to the next task.

My meditation and energy training at *The Self Realization Centre* taught me that we need different kinds of energy to perform different tasks. For example, attending a meeting, working with clients and eating lunch with colleagues all call for diverse energies. We learned to take a short break and to mentally clear ourselves before going on to the next activity. Walking around the block, breathing deeply, washing our hands or visualizing our energy field seamlessly circling our body can all renew us.

Are women groomed to be caregivers?

Some of us between the ages of forty and sixty lived in an environment that taught us how to be a caring woman. I, like others in my age group, received mixed messages about getting a good education, while still putting family first.

---

[1] Reprinted by permission of the author

My mother, being an old-fashioned woman in many ways, instilled two rules in me both overtly and covertly: always put your family first, and have a small job on the side - not a career – one that lends itself to the family's schedule. However, by the time I entered the workforce, expectations were that women would have careers as well as families. It is true that we can be anything we want, *but we can't do it all simultaneously.*

An interesting German study found that the entire life history of a sample of women predisposed them to care for their mothers. They developed a feeling of responsibility and caring toward their mother long before caregiving was needed and later expressed this by providing them with increasing help.

This impulse to be a caregiver that develops in some of us through our lifetime as a daughter may be magnified by specific events that take place in a family. My father died when he was only fifty-four, leaving my mother a widow at age fifty-three. Although mom functioned well in the world and had an interesting, reasonably well paying job, she was quite emotionally dependent.

After my father died, my mother-in-law warned me, in her gentle, knowing way, not to make myself a martyr over the tragedy of his early death. Elda knew well what she was talking about. As the only daughter of a Southern Ontario farm family she had been at the beck and call of her widowed, arthritic mother for many years. What Elda said helped me with boundaries, but I still felt a keen sense of responsibility for my mother's happiness in many ways, despite our bumpy relationship.

My empathy for my mother's situation grew over the next few years as I experienced other painful events in my own life. My first marriage ended, then I met and had a child with my current partner, a baby girl who lived for only two days. We were blessed with another girl two years later and my partner, my mother and I doted on her. My mother's and my lives became more intertwined now that I was a parent. As I write this, I realize that these events, along with my earlier conditioning as a daughter, prepared me to be my mother's caregiver later on.

Many expectations of ourselves

When I was working as a Trager bodywork practitioner in the mid-nineties, two different colleagues I visited for healing sessions said to me, "End your day when you could still give one or two more sessions. You have to have something left for yourself."

Being a caregiver is a lot like that. As caregivers we often give and give *until we have nothing left to give*, and certainly nothing left over for ourselves. Then we often become burned out in body, mind and spirit.

- Operating on 'automatic pilot', not really noticing what we've done during our day, is a sign of burnout.
- Dissociation, or feeling like we're not fully in our body can be another sign.

The internal calling of midlife

Midlife offers us a great opportunity to come into our fullness… a chance to become more of who we truly are. If we keep our life moving at a daunting pace, denying ourselves the gift of time, we interfere with this process.

In my work with women from all walks of life, I've noticed a common theme. We often don't recognize that we have much more choice over how to live our lives than we know.

- The decision to take care of our personal needs is acceptable.
- If we ignore this extraordinary midlife opportunity to get to know ourselves in new ways, we lose out.

It's not only the chance to enrich ourselves that is lost. When we don't slow down, go within and prioritize, we may develop stress-related health issues like depleted adrenals, low thyroid, chronic fatigue, or heart problems.

Boundaries – theirs and yours

- Our relationship with our parent is a complex emotional one layered with history.
- It is crucial that we clarify for ourselves *what we're doing for them*, and *why we're doing it*.

Most of us love our parents, we want to honor them and what they did for us. Even though we're adults we still want to please them. Our strong emotional bond, combined with the implicit and explicit demands our aging parents put on us and we *put on ourselves*, means that expectations for us as caregivers are too high. The boundary lines between ourselves and our parent become blurred over time and it's hard for us to tell where their needs end and our needs begin.

Those of us with challenging parental relationships find interactions are often complicated. My mother and I have had some good times over the years, and in our own way we've been close, but the relationship has been difficult for me until recently. An unexpected gift of her disease has been that she has let go of much of her anxiety and of the edge that allowed her to survive in life. As she progressed in her dementia, mom slowly moved into a quieter, more peaceful place. I no longer felt criticized by her and we are now close, connecting in both non-verbal and verbal ways.

Examining the motivation behind our caregiving will help us be clear about our actions. Knowing *why* we're doing *what* we're doing helps us to function with clarity rather than simply reacting.

Our beliefs

All of us operate under a set of beliefs we've held for a long time, called our *'belief system'*. Much of our belief system helps us tremendously, but some parts of it can be quite detrimental to our well-being.

Another way to look at this is to think about the stories that underlie our beliefs. Many of my counseling instructors were *Narrative Therapists*. The idea behind this therapy is that we all have stories we tell ourselves that are not working for us - ones that make our lives more difficult - called *'Problem Saturated Stories'*. We can rework them into positive stories that more closely represent the way we want to live. These *'Preferred Stories'* embody our hopes and our dreams. In coaching we use many symbolic and introspective techniques to rewrite the stories that no longer serve us, so we can live the lives we all long for and deserve to have.

- A Canadian government *Centres of Excellence* study found that women who felt positive about caregiving were far less stressed.
- These women differed from the women with major stress because they drew on strong personal and community support networks, and were knowledgeable about the programs and services available.
- The women believed they had a right to support and services.

What enabled them to feel less stressed, I wonder? Perhaps their internal dialogue… their story about caregiving helped them feel more empowered.

Pacing ourselves

Joan Borton, author of *Drawing from the Women's Well*, says pacing ourselves is key in midlife. I completely agree with this. It is something I've practiced since my early thirties when I was introduced to the concept. I built on it with my formal meditation training at the Self Realization Centre, where we were taught how to change and clear our energy before beginning different activities.

Pacing is new to many women. Many of us are used to pushing our bodies mercilessly in order to perform the myriad functions and roles of our lives. When we push ourselves so hard we go into overload and our life begins to spin out of control. We've all felt this way at times. Borton refers to this out-of-touch feeling as *'emotional blackout'*.

I truly believe that midlife is an opportunity for enormous growth. It is a time when we are meant to come into our fullness. Midlife women have so much wisdom… wisdom gained from all our life experience. We can take this and meld it with our newfound passion for change that is the gift of our midlife. From this solid, grounded place we can focus on what really moves us.

Chapter 3 - How We Change in MidLife

In coaching we often ask our clients what they would be like if their stressful thoughts miraculously disappeared from their heads. Most women reply that they would feel freer, more energetic, more joyful and so on. But some struggle with the idea and can't conceive of eliminating the troublesome thoughts. I explain to them that without the negative thoughts taking up so much of our attention, we can focus on new and empowering endeavors.

Midlife reminds me of this coaching exercise. After we transcend the challenges of our mid years and arrive at the door marked *'menopause'*, we're not the same as we were before. We have left some things behind and gained a whole new world of possibilities. Our basic character and personality remain, but now we have a *different presence* in the world. The profound physiological changes that have taken place over the past several years have shaken us up in body, mind and spirit.

For many women, turning fifty is something to be celebrated, not hidden. Some women take a special holiday with friends, others spend some quiet time away by themselves. I had a wonderful party in a little house by the sea for my fiftieth. I'd completed the first year of my counseling program, and was one year into menopause. The future felt promising, I had a sense of purpose.

A unique situation

Now that there are so many of us reaching this phase of our lives, we're searching for answers – in the media, from the internet and through conversations with other women - answers that validate and explain what we're going through. I for one, am glad to be part of a group that has a growing voice as we age.

In the past, researchers ignored women's midlife for the most part, because historically women died younger, most doctors were men, they applied male study results to women and, most importantly, there was a stigma around female aging.

Many other cultures celebrate menopause as a time when a woman is moving into a deeper level of self-discovery and spiritual awareness, and older women are looked to for guidance. In our western society the perceived imperfection implicit in female aging is now beginning to break down as more of us step forward and become vocal.

Something happens to us...

We begin to view things in a new light as we change within. The things we've always done and the way we've done them may no longer work for us now. We want something different and we begin to question what that might be and to take steps to put our desires into action.

Our gradual hormonal realignment combined with our natural maturing as females means we're often more in touch with what we want and need as individuals. Our focus changes from other-oriented to a more internal emphasis, and we're able to bring increased clarity to our lives and our interactions with others.

As our yearnings unfold, so do plans for the future. We start to feel that life is short, so there's an urgency to take action that wasn't there before.

- Our biology actually helps us to take better care of ourselves in the midlife years.
- The drive to look after our family and others becomes less intense as our hormones change.
- We're also not as interested in conflict avoidance as when we were younger.
- For some women the experience feels like a fog is lifting.

I've personally noticed this type of gradual change over the past thirteen years as I continue to express more of my unique self.

Dr. Christiane Northrup, well-known author of *The Wisdom of Menopause*, says we experience a *circuitry rewiring* during perimenopause, one that affects all systems of our body, especially the part of the brain where strong emotions originate. This can account for the intense and sometimes changeable feelings we experience, and for our passionate desire to speak out about and act on our new ideas and ambitions.

How our intuition can helps us

We all have intuition. Businessmen call it a '*hunch*', therapists call it '*instinct*', or '*a sense*'.

It often expands in midlife, and many women notice significant increases in their intuitive insights around these years. We feel a sense of sureness when we follow this internal guidance.

We can use our intuition in any area of our lives when we're making decisions and interacting with others. It can help us get a sense of how our parent is feeling emotionally as well as physically. I use it all the time with my mother, often without even realizing it. When we tune in to and heed the subtle messages coming from this part of our brain, a whole new world may emerge for us.

Dealing with many emotions

In the midlife transition we sometimes find our emotions are closer to the surface than before. They come in many guises, appearing as sadness or depression at times, or maybe anger or confusion at others. We're not used to having such immediate feelings, and they can be annoying and upsetting when they intrude on our lives.

Emotions are simply energy held as tension in specific places in our bodies. They give us information about our internal process so we can choose how we want to respond. In coaching we often look to the body to tell us what is really going on inside us.

Feelings are signals worth listening to. They may be telling us something is not right - perhaps we're avoiding an issue or compromising ourselves too much in our caregiving or other relationships.

Many of us experience some depression as we're transforming profoundly in our body, mind and spirit. When my friend Diane and I were going through perimenopause, most of the literature told us it wasn't normal to feel depressed, but we knew better. Recent research says mild depression is common at this time.

I have learned from personal and professional experience that it takes a lot of energy to keep our thoughts and feelings hidden, and that this is actually much harder on us. Giving ourselves both the time and the permission to experience our emotions is important. We live in a 'get over it and get on with it society', but in fact a quiet cry can be a good release, or coffee with a friend who lets us vent can be cleansing. Expressing our feelings helps us to move forward.

The practical and emotional demands of caregiving may amplify our existing depression. Seeking professional help is one way to deal with emotions that feel too complicated and confusing. Outside input from a trained, experienced person can be an enormous support and comfort at a time like this.

The midlife years are when we let go of the past and grieve for what was. We shed many things, including the image of our parents as they were. Our strong emotions are normal responses to what we're going through.

With the passing of time things change, and when we allow this change to unfold we move ahead in our lives. We come to know our parent, and they us, in a deeper way through the gift of this experience.

Our changing identities & priorities

We may yearn to make over one or more areas of our lives; some of us even begin life anew by following our personal passions and goals. Dr. Christiane Northrup personally experienced such intense yearning in midlife she felt she must '*grow or die*'. She went on to become a health spokesperson and teacher for many thousands of midlife women.

In midlife we begin to uncover aspects of ourselves and dreams for our future that have been there all along, rather than creating actual new personalities. We're becoming more comfortable with our personal power now and many of us feel more proactive about taking charge of the direction of our lives. We may express our newfound sense of self by seeking like-minded people, beginning new projects, traveling around the world or acting on the desire to relax and simply be. Our changes also mean we're able to speak our minds to our loved ones more, to maintain good boundaries, and not feel guilty about doing so.

Going inward to find solitude

- We can sense the changes taking place in us even though we can't see them.
- A major passage requires attention to our physical, emotional and spiritual needs.

Solitude is not the same as loneliness. It is a quiet enjoyment of our own company. I believe it's an acquired taste, like the taste of a fine wine. When I was about forty, I began to teach myself to enjoy being alone without my busy '*monkey mind*', as the Buddhist's call it, disturbing me with its constant barrage of busyness and recriminations.

In our earlier years we're more outward-oriented, by midlife the desire to move inward begins. Judith Duerk, my mentor during my forties, taught me about women's need to go inward at this time to find their true selves. I learned to reconnect with myself by quietly going inside and finding my center.

- A knowing and a sureness will arise out of the space we've carved for ourselves.
- Unscheduled quiet time will help us get a clearer perspective on everything.

When we allow ourselves to quietly contemplate, we may be surprised at the rich ideas that emerge from within us. From my introspection came the desire to work with women in new ways, and I began a graduate program in counseling in Vancouver.

When we're so immersed in the process of being a caregiver, this quiet time may seem like a luxury. In fact, it could be a key to recharging ourselves, especially before or after time spent with our parent. If we make this practice part of our day it will become as important to us as breathing before long.

Taking the risk to answer our internal call

We can choose whether to bring our new identities out into the world or not, and to what extent. It depends on the intensity of the social pressures around us and on whether we're willing and able to make tough decisions.

Our culture and our families tend to assume females will be the ones to care for others, and when women begin their personal exploration it sometimes causes conflict. We have the task of not only challenging our own thinking around caregiving, but also of dealing with the expectations of others.

It requires courage and vigilance to heed the call of our internal voice. The pressures to '*go along with the program*' are often quite subtle and we may not realize we're being influenced by them. Consequently the *internal messages we're getting may be very faint*, drowned out by the noise of life's busyness.

If we're even able to hear our internal messages, we may judge ourselves for feeling this way. Even if we want to, we're not sure we can stop what we're doing when the needs of our aging parents, our work and other family members overshadow everything else in our lives. But with patience, a good support system and our newly developed skills, we can change our priorities.

- '*Turtle steps*' are small tasks that we can do easily and comfortably, without frightening our brain into a *fight or flight state*. (from Martha Beck's teachings)
- When we use turtle steps to make change, we'll keep moving forward and get gradual and consistent results.
- Our change will be lasting when we live this way.

Giving ourselves permission

Living a vibrant, joyful life means achieving balance in all areas. An important part of this delicate balance is ensuring that we ourselves flourish while also being accountable to others in our lives.

Many of us feel changed at our core. Caring for our parent in their latter years is part of the transition, and it involves a process of growing into fuller adulthood for many of us. We have now become the generation in charge, the glue that holds our family together. As we watch our parent decline over a period of time, we confront our own mortality and what that means to us personally.

- It is our right to invite creative change it into our lives.

- When we allow ourselves to step back and prioritize, we're able to take the necessary steps to achieve our parent's well-being *while also thriving and growing ourselves.*

If we don't exercise our right, we may feel regret and resentment for a life not fully lived. Shirley Valentine, in the play by that name, says it well:

> "So I said to her, 'Jane, why is it that there's all this unused life?'... It's the same for everyone... what kills us is the terrible weight of all this unused life that we carry round."[2]
>
> Willy Russell

---

[2] Reprinted by permission of the author

Chapter 4 – How Our Relationships Change

Now that we've gone through some of midlife's changes, we begin to view ourselves and our lives in a new light. As some of our old beliefs give way to new, empowering ones, our internal changes begin to be reflected in all we do in the world.

- The new, empowering stories we're telling ourselves and our new behaviors flowing from them impact all aspects of our lives.
- When we change there is a domino effect that touches everyone we're close to, changing each relationship.

Our social roles
- Our society tells us how we're supposed to act in group situations.
- These behaviors are part of our social roles.
- In some ways our roles are similar to what actors do when they play a part.

We learn from a young age to play roles. Many of them have been given to us by others who are more powerful than us. These are called '*ascribed roles*'. For example, as a reader of this book you likely have the ascribed role of daughter, as I do. '*Achieved roles*', on the other hand, are roles we have chosen to play and have taken actions to initiate. For example, I went back to school in midlife to study counseling.

In every society, women and men are forced into different social roles because of the obvious biological difference between them. Roles shape our attitudes and behaviors and often limit us.

- There's nothing wrong with roles but when we get too caught up in them they become harmful.
- A role is only some of our characteristics, not the totality of who we are.

We may lose ourselves in our roles completely if we get overly involved in playing them to perfection. We may forget who we are as individuals and in our drive to be everything to everyone, the uniqueness that makes up each woman may be lost.

Changing roles
Perhaps while we were raising children we chose a particular lifestyle that provided emotional and economic stability for our family. Maybe we ignored some things that didn't support or nurture us personally over the years for the good of the whole.

Many midlife women feel a strong desire for their own private space where they can just 'be' themselves. By mid-perimenopause, I craved personal space so badly, I longed for the solitude of a cabin in the woods.

In reality, I was unwilling to completely step out of my roles of wife and mother. I did, however, spend lots of time by myself. I raised only one child and by this time she was moving into her later teens, so there was very little hands-on parenting required.

I enjoyed my walks around our quiet neighborhood, where just stepping out the door means being surrounded by enormous coniferous trees. I felt so pulled inward that mostly I wanted to hide away and to rest. Whatever your particular need is, it's important to identify it for yourself and then act on it as much as possible.

Intimate relationships

Intimate relationships change in midlife. Some of our marriages deteriorate completely, some become stagnant, while others reach a new level of satisfaction and awareness.

We feel differently about all our relationships by midlife. When we are stressed, we don't have the patience to work through differences in a marriage that's not running smoothly. If we're overloaded by the demands of caregiving for our parents, as well as with work and our personal life, we're probably looking for support from our partner.

I've met many women in the process of separating from their partners or who need radical improvements in their relationship in order stay in it. From reading mixed gender blogs, it seems that the processes men and women go through at midlife magnify their gender differences, with women urgently trying to make sense of the changes going on in them, while the men seem more content as things are. This disconnect reminds me of John Grey's *Men Are from Mars, Women Are from Venus* metaphor.

We know what we want

- By midlife many women feel more complete in themselves. Now that our nurturing hormones are depleted we may even resent looking after our families or caregiving for our parents.

As surprising as this may sound to younger women, in midlife we often develop a take it or leave it attitude about spending time with close friends. This is because the pleasure centers of our brains are no longer stimulated the way they were previously by natural chemicals.

- Our thinking and our feelings are usually clearer.

- We may feel more balanced and grounded within ourselves without fluctuations from hormones.

Many of us feel it's time to explore new interests, revive old ones, to travel or to simply spend quality time alone whenever we wish to. Beginning caregiving duties for an aging parent or intensifying existing duties may therefore come at what seems like an inappropriate time in our life.

The reluctant caregiver

Many women anticipate caring for their aging parents in the future, and do so with mixed emotions. Some of us look forward to lovingly repaying past kindness, while others dread increasing their involvement with difficult parents.

- A new kind of relationship emerges with our parent in their declining years. In some ways the parent becomes the child of their adult child as the years go on.

Around the time my mother moved from Victoria to the Sunshine Coast to be closer to us, I had several dreams about her. In the dreams she was called 'my little mommy'. She's a tiny woman, but I'd never thought of her in that way before, as she's always been a powerhouse. In each dream my partner, myself and sometimes our daughter were rescuing her from danger. In one dream, she fell off a dock into the ocean, and we pulled her out. Her tininess was a different kind of smallness in my dreams… a child-like one, a precursor of what was to come.

The challenges & frustrations of eldercare

When we traveled from North Vancouver to the Sunshine Coast to take my mother out for lunch, it took well over an hour to help her through her washroom preparations and dressing, and sometimes I got restless. The more I pushed, the slower she went. I believe it was one of her few opportunities to take some limited control over her life.

- Communication issues between us and our parent may become magnified now.
- Interactions with them may bring added stress in the form of old emotional baggage.

Becoming truly separate from our parent

Sometimes a parent is critical, rude or abusive to their adult child and it's hard not to take it personally. Experts often advise us to separate the speaker from the speech, because it is their illness talking, not them. This could be true in some cases, but other times it could simply be the parent's normal personality emerging, perhaps in a less monitored form than before.

- It takes some of us longer to fully separate from our parent than others, perhaps well into our adult years.

I went through a long process of separating from my mother and becoming my own person. As I grew up, and even into my adult years, she figured prominently in my life. It seemed mom always knew how I should live my life, and her ideas usually differed from my game plan! It created an adversarial situation; I reacted to what I took to be criticism from her, and her occasional comparisons of me to higher achieving peers felt hurtful.

- Many of us have boundary issues with our parents.
- We can teach ourselves to put firm boundaries around our interactions with our parent.
- This new relationship won't happen overnight, but it's quite doable.

By the time my mother moved into her first care home, I was well along in my separation from her and felt quite empowered. We had a couple of false starts early on, then I was able to deal with her firmly and clearly when necessary, which was extremely satisfying.

Mom felt uprooted initially in care and this translated into anxiety and irritability at times. Twice when I arrived she shook her finger at me, saying "Where have you been?" in the intimidating *'mother voice'* she used when I was a child. I could feel myself shrinking inside until I felt about two and a half feet tall! The third time this happened I replied, "If you do that again, I'm leaving right now." Mom immediately stopped her behavior and it never happened again, despite her advanced dementia. At the same time I was careful to reassure her that I would always come back to see her.

- You're not alone in your struggles with your parent.
- By being clear with them about what you're willing and able to do and tolerate, you'll develop boundaries that your parent will respond to.

You have taken on the responsibility of caregiving to help your parent - not to exhaust and deplete yourself. It's an opportunity to ensure that your parent is looked after *well enough - it doesn't have to be perfect.*

Taking the next steps

Clarity in our dealings with our parent is important. We're already making decisions for them, or helping them with decision making on a regular basis. Eventually we may be responsible for questions of life and death for our parent. When we're emotionally calm and centered it's much easier to think clearly and to make the best decisions.

Through coming to terms with family issues, we won't expend unnecessary energy feeling upset, angry or resentful. Putting our parental issues to rest means we heal ourselves and our relationship with them.

Feeling unlike our usual adult selves around our parent at times is not at all uncommon. Most of us often feel a bit younger when we're with our parents; remnants of this remain with us our whole lives.

When we stop to think about it, it makes sense. The connection with our mother in particular is a profound one. Why wouldn't we feel vulnerability and have a desire to please when we're around that all-powerful figure… the one who was responsible for our very survival from the moment we were born?

If you have a rocky relationship with your parent, ask yourself: "How old do I feel when I'm dealing with my Mom or Dad? The answer to this question may vary widely from time to time. Perhaps you feel completely your adult self most of the time, and you're occasionally triggered by what's said or done. Or maybe you always feel younger than your years when you're with your parent.

If you notice you're feeling kid-like around your parent at times, or maybe you're angry, frustrated or resentful, consider asking yourself, "Why am I behaving this way?".

When our relationship with our parent is too fraught with difficulty, the bottom line is:

- We do our best to contain our feelings so we can put *basic services* in place for the safety and security of our elder.
- No more is really called for if we feel our relationship can't be repaired.

We may even choose not to have contact with our parent at all if our past trauma makes it impossible for us to attend to their needs or even to be around them. *Many women feel this way*. We have a right to do what's best for us - regardless of what others may think – we're the only ones qualified to make this decision. We need not feel guilty about it. It may help to talk to someone we trust, such as a counselor, spiritual advisor, partner, or friend.

Powerful feelings are normal
- Watching our strong and capable parent age is not an easy thing.
- We often feel a mixture of feelings such as sadness, regret… even depression at times.
- It's normal to go through a range of emotions.
- When we acknowledge and honor our painful and often confusing feelings, we move through them and experience a sense of relief and peace ultimately.

I still feel emotionally off-kilter at times when I visit my mother on Sundays. I usually take her out for a while and then spend time with her in the care home. We relax, look at pictures, I ensure she's well hydrated with tea and water, sometimes I oil her scalp for her, or do whatever else needs doing. Although I feel comfortable and relaxed in the slow pace of the care center, and am getting to know many of the old folks, it's still not easy to see so many very elderly people all in one place, and know that my mother is one of them.

Sibling rivalry anyone?

In addition to our relationship with our parent and all it entails, many of us have the added challenge of relating to our siblings with respect to our parent's care (unless we're an only child with its own inherent challenges).

- Usually one adult child takes on most of the responsibility for parental care.
- Many caregivers say the biggest source of their relational stress is their siblings.

You may find your brother or sister does not want to become deeply involved in the care of your parent, or they may have their own agenda for parental care, and may perceive your input as interference.

My brother and I have collaborated in the care of our mother, but haven't always formally planned what each would do. One of us stepped forward at various stages of mom's care and did what was needed. In our case this has worked out in a very positive way. Mom has been well cared for, and we've done it all with very little friction.

It's not unusual for adult siblings to relate to each other as they did when they were young when dealing with their parent's care. Perhaps old emotions are triggered by unconscious sibling competition from bygone days. This can make co-operative decision making difficult.

As the primary caregiver, we often expect our less involved siblings to know what is needed without being asked. After all, it's their parent too, isn't it? When they don't respond the way we think they should, we may feel resentful.

Sometimes when we do ask our siblings for help, we're not specific in our requests and they aren't clear about what we want them to do. They may not always ask for clarification, and then things don't get done.

Claire Berman stresses that it is important for us, as the primary caregiver, to honestly check in with ourselves to see if we could be contributing to our sibling taking a smaller role in our parent's care. For example, are we being controlling? Are we unconsciously trying to be the child who is closest to the parent?

Final thoughts

It's often better for our parent and for us to spend a moderate amount of high quality time together, rather than for us to feel obligated to continually attend to their needs; this is a very personal choice.

My friend Camilla, who had an extremely elderly father and a husband living in separate care homes, told me she realized over time that their care facility was their home and they were quite content there. She then felt more comfortable with the choices she had made and didn't feel she needed to be with them all the time.

- If you choose to be a caregiver for your parent, appreciate the time spent with them and make it as pleasant as possible.
- We can only enjoy our parent, and they us, if we are meeting our own needs.

I have a scheduled visit with my mother once a week, and sometimes a second visit when I have an appointment in her town or she comes to our house. I'm slowly coming to terms with leaving her for longer periods of time as we follow our dreams of traveling and volunteering. I feel reassured that she is safe and very well cared for.

We enjoy being together, with our limited conversations and our frequent laughter. I feel peaceful when I'm with her… somehow nurtured. She's still my mom, even if she can't string her sentences together properly anymore.

A story about children & parents

Recently I wrote a blog post about midlife caregiving that was partially inspired by Robert Munsch's story '*Love You Forever*'. I'm reprinting it here as I think it encapsulates the essence of our lives as midlife caregivers to our aging parents:

> *I'll love you forever,*
> *I'll like you for always,*
> *as long as I'm living*
> *my baby you'll be."* [3]
> by Robert Munsch
>
> The Sunday before last I was pushing my mother along the sidewalk in her wheelchair to Starbucks, where we often go for tea. She can walk, but not quite that far roundtrip. On the way we passed a young mom pushing her small daughter in a stroller. We all smiled

---

[3] Reprinted by permission of the author.

at each other. In the moment after our encounter I 'got' the symbolism of it and I sensed the young mom did too.

Life's a circle game as Joni Mitchell sang. I take care of my aging mom and the young mom we passed on the street takes care of her little girl. One day her girl may take care of her. Then I thought of Robert Munsch's story *'Love You Forever'*.

Always one of my favourite authors, we heard Munsch tell his stories in Belleville, Ontario in 1989. *Love You Forever* was one of them. It's a story about a mother who raises her son, then when she's very, very old, he takes care of her. He shows his love for her in a very unique way by climbing a ladder up to her bedroom, climbing in through the window, then picking his old mom up and rocking her gently in her rocking chair. Munsch told us whenever he tells this story the children all laugh and the parents cry. It's been years since I read the story but the images are still with me and I feel deeply moved.

In the circle of time parents look after children, and sometimes children look after their parents. Most women in midlife do not have our aging parents living with us, but many of us are hands-on caregivers. Some of us are professional caregivers in addition to caregiving for our spouses, our children and our aging parents.

It's a challenging job and often a very emotional experience to stand by our parents as they diminish mentally and physically. We take on this additional responsibility as a labor of love, as a duty or as a combination of the two.
    July 2008
    From MidLife Maze[4]

---

[4] Reprinted by permission of the author.

Chapter 5 - Thoughts That Run the Show

The stress epidemic

A stress management lecturer explained to his audience the long-term effects of stress by holding a glass of water in the air and asking them to guess the weight of it. The answers from the audience varied widely, of course. The lecturer explained to them that the actual weight of the glass of water didn't matter; what was significant was how long the glass was held up in the air.

This metaphor for looking at long-term stress applies very well to us as caregivers. Whether we care for our parent full time in our home or live a thousand miles away, the responsibility for their well-being is always with us. The emotional and psychological stress is harder on us than the actual physical caregiving.

- Our stressful thoughts make an already challenging situation more difficult.
- When we deal with this problematic thinking we'll feel better in all ways.

Since we're in this for the long haul it's important for our health that we develop ways to tame our thoughts, refresh ourselves and off-load some of our responsibilities.

Sadly, many of us are on overload much of the time. As our society ramps up its tempo we're bombarded with an enormous amount of stimulus from outside. At the same time we're also experiencing a *constant internal monologue*. Buddhists call it our '*monkey mind*'. Steven Hayes calls this struggle with our thoughts and the resultant feelings '*the mind train*'.

The stress effect

- I've learned that when our heads are occupied with stressful thoughts it's difficult to care for ourselves well because we can't focus clearly on our needs.
- The hormone cortisol is released into our bodies in times of stress and our immune system and our whole health are negatively affected.

When our mind runs the show

Out of the thousands of thoughts going through our mind daily, we choose some of them as our truth. These thoughts then become our beliefs. While some of our beliefs help us, unfortunately many are stressful, limiting and/or negative. I've worked long and hard at dissolving my own limiting beliefs, and feel certain I'm gaining ground with them. They are very subtle and quite insidious, often hard to catch hold of.

The thoughts and beliefs that tell us we have to be everything give us *'stress overload'*. When our mind dictates what we should or shouldn't be doing, we often experience uproar in our heads. This makes it hard for us to identify and take the steps we need to fulfill ourselves as well as nurture others.

Often we wish there were more hours in each day so we could get everything done, but the things that are really important to us *will* get done. Lack of time is actually a perception on our part; it is something our mind does. It happens very easily when we don't take control of our thinking.

When we develop the habit of slowing ourselves down and breathing deeply on a regular basis throughout the day, things seems clearer to us. We become more mindful of everything, including how we want to spend our available time. Once we've dealt with our stressful and sometimes unrealistic expectations of ourselves, *we'll find there is enough time for whatever we decide to make our priority*.

What I learned about calming my mind

One morning I sat on my back porch sipping my morning coffee, and I thought, "I don't know where to begin today". I had a lot going on in my business, plus my self-assigned summer chores of outside painting, upkeep of my flower garden and entertaining my mother, arriving by handy-dart bus the next day.

For some reason I didn't have a written or mental 'to do list' that day. My anxiety took over and my mind began its game of uproar. I felt overwhelmed and began beating myself up, saying, "You can't do it all", "You'll never be successful", and so on.

As I sat there I glanced up at the giant coniferous trees in the tiny forest behind the house. Gazing at the trees calmed me, and something shifted subtly inside as I began to feel the peace. I automatically breathed deeply and felt myself meld with the tranquil scene around me. Through the quiet, a thought presented itself to me: *"This is what counts, not all this internal rushing and agitation"*.

Suddenly I realized there was a bird sitting at the very top of one high tree, another one lower down, and a third lower still. When the top bird stretched its head fully out so it was pointing skyward, I saw that it was a blue heron. The second bird flew away suddenly and I could see that it was a small eagle. The third revealed itself as another heron.

I was moved seeing these very special birds; it felt like a privilege being in their presence. I later learned that blue herons symbolize following your heart in doing what feels right for you, no matter what others may say, while the message of the eagle is to combine your wisdom with your courage. I've seen '*my birds*' several times since that day, and last week three eagles flew in the sky over my home.

Scratching the word 'should' from our vocabulary

- Do you find things seem harder when your schedule is overloaded and you're juggling several tasks at once?
- Recent brain research shows that multitasking and over-scheduling lead to out of control thoughts.
- Dr. Lee Pulos, a cutting-edge BC psychologist, told me that our brains are rewiring themselves because we're all multitasking so much.

Stopping our *mind train* and controlling our tendency to over-schedule may sound easier said than done, but it is quite possible depending on the priorities we set. If our thinking tells us: "*I must…*", or "*I should*", we can challenge it! Don't assume you must do something "*just because…*". You can give yourself permission to make a completely different choice.

We call this approach '*out of the box thinking*' in our coaching practice. Where is it written in stone that we must do so many things? When something inside us screams "*stop*", our body, mind and spirit are sending out a very strong message.

- Let's challenge the thoughts and beliefs we hold about our '*shoulds*'.
- When we eliminate '*shoulds*' and '*musts*', we're then ready to clarify what we truly want and need to do. What emerges may be most surprising. Try it and see.

Could it be that much of what you're doing out of duty or habit could be done by others or even eliminated entirely? Perhaps someone else would be happy to take on a volunteer job or to earn some money caregiving. In the case of a sibling, they might welcome the opportunity to spend more time with their parent *if we step back*. Our children and our partners are probably quite capable of taking on many more responsibilities than we've given them credit for.

There's no simple, across-the-board answer for dealing with the duties that sometimes feel like a super-human burden. Challenging the thoughts and beliefs that demand we over-perform will lift this load. Now the change has already begun!

No one will do this for us. We must act for ourselves. We are the only ones who can make the choices about our lives… the choices that are right for *us*. When we *act* rather than *react* to the needs and requests of others, we will discover satisfying ways to live in interdependence with them… ways that bring us joy.

When I sat still and really noticed the amazing natural beauty of the birds and the trees outside my back door, it made an enormous difference to me. The difference wasn't just for that day; it is for each one of my days.

I *invite you* to make the choice to *stop* your activities frequently throughout your day to rejuvenate yourself and to clarify your next steps. When you feel drawn to take a pause, or if you feel yourself moving away from your center, just *stop*. Take a break, breathe deeply, get some fresh air, drink water, stretch your body, or eat something nourishing. In short, do whatever refreshes and replenishes you. In this way you will return yourself to that solid grounded place within. Give yourself this gift whenever possible.

Chapter 6 - Taking Care of You

When we travel by plane, the flight attendant always demonstrates the procedure to follow in an emergency. If the cabin of the plane loses compression and the oxygen masks fall down, put your own mask on first, then help the young, the old, the sick or the injured put theirs on. If we don't have enough oxygen, if we don't look after ourselves first, then we'll be of no use to those around us.

Caregiving for our elderly parent is exactly the same. We can't be of use to them unless we take care of ourselves. We need breathing room, and that includes the time and space to look after our own needs. Not just our basic needs of food, water and sleep, but our emotional, psychological and spiritual ones… the ones that make the difference between merely existing and thriving.

- Think back to the last time you let yourself do exactly what you wanted.
- Do you remember how long ago that was?
- How much time did you spend on your chosen activity?

In our busy world often each moment of our day is accounted for, with no uncommitted time available to us. Leisure originally meant time that was free from duty, but over the years we've changed the meaning. When we're overbooked, our leisure time often isn't free at all. Because we feel guilty when we don't get everything done, we fill up our spare time with what we *perceive* as necessary activities. For example we might say to ourselves: "*I must work out*" or "*I owe Mercedes a phone call.*"

Where to start?

Once we begin to deliberately notice our actions, our change has already begun. We're becoming more aware of what causes us stress, and we can change our patterns.

We can gradually train ourselves out of the habit of over-scheduling. When we put ourselves in charge of setting our priorities, we can control the pace we move at. *We must be proactive about our needs*; nothing will change if we put *everything* and *everyone's* needs first.

As we consciously choose positive thoughts our brain will develop healthier habits. Our new ways of thinking will support us in our changes and help us feel more peaceful.

Recognizing the 'MidLife' you

The reality of our over-scheduled lives combined with our body's biological changes puts high demands on us on all levels. Caregiving for our aging parent means we divide ourselves, our energy and our time even more.

- The midlife transition puts an extra strain on us in all ways.
- We're at a disadvantage if we begin these years rundown.
- Minimizing our stress in midlife will help us.

Most of us probably feel psychologically unprepared when it comes to midlife. We don't anticipate the changes that are starting; we didn't think they'd be happening yet. When I was forty-five, I thought of myself as relatively young, so it was quite a surprise to realize that my body was beginning the process of becoming an older woman!

Along with the commonplace shortened menstrual cycles and lighter periods, I began to notice an allover tightness in my body, more frequent headaches, sleep loss, weight gain and, curiously, poor coordination (like I had in early pregnancy). My mother, my friend Diane and my Jin-shin-do practitioner all told me I was experiencing symptoms of perimenopause.

Being the type of person who embraces new experiences, after my initial surprise, I began to look at perimenopause as an adventure. I found myself intrigued with the mysterious process going on inside me that caused me to feel so unlike myself. My intuition grew, and my desires seemed to flow more from a heart-felt place, and less from my left brain than before. As time passed I realized that what I wanted was to live from my passions instead of my '*shoulds*'.

Many women make a decision to live their lives more purposefully around this time, perhaps you're one of them. With time we all come to a place of peace with the 'new' us. We learn how unimportant some of life's minor irritations are and concentrate on what is truly meaningful to each of us. We also no longer strive for that illusive perfection in everything we do. We start to let go.

This all reflects in our caregiving, as we take each day and each moment with our parent, and just enjoy the here and now of being with them.

Feeling invigorated

- To feel really good inside and out taking care of our basic physical needs is a must.
- Good quality food, plenty of water, adequate sleep, fresh air, and exercise that suits our abilities, interests and energies are important.
- We'll feel our best physically and mentally and experience a sense of well-being when we get plenty of rest and leisure.

By checking in with ourselves at intervals of fifteen to thirty minutes, we can reset our trajectory when needed, and keep in balance. Simple things like replenishing ourselves with water or food, taking a moment to breathe, meditate, or to walk around the block can make a positive difference to our day.

Try this: Take a deep breath in, exhale slowly, then ask yourself: *"What do I need right this moment?"*. You'll be surprised at how quickly the answer will come. Honor your wisdom by responding to what your body-mind-spirit is asking for.

- It's all about balance - the more often we tune in to ourselves, the more we'll feel 'in the flow'. It's as simple as that.

Sleep isn't a luxury
- Many of us are sleep deprived now.
- We get less than the recommended seven to nine hours sleep a night.

Sleep has become almost a luxury for many people. We use the extra time to fit in more chores, put in more hours at work, care for our parent, or maybe to socialize. I've known women who stay up until three or four a.m. sewing or writing, stealing private time away from the demands of their daytime life.

We're often more sensitive to interrupted sleep in midlife, and sometimes our internal fluctuations make getting enough rest a problem. We may have trouble going to sleep, or may awaken during the night and stay awake. Chinese medical theory says that not being able to sleep when we need, or feeling too sleepy during daytime hours is caused by a particular system being out of balance. There are many natural products available to women now in addition to pharmaceuticals to help with this.

Moving our bodies
- How we exercise is a very individual thing.
- We need a method that really appeals to us.

I'm not an athletic person, and my main form of exercise in the past has been gentle walking. My partner encouraged me to find something I really enjoyed so I would stay with it. After many years I've found that a holistic, dance-based aerobic class is the right thing for me. But as much as I enjoy it, the idea of staying home and vegging sometimes appeals more.

When I don't move my body enough my system seems to clog up, and my feeling of well-being is replaced by one of heaviness. I talked to my acupuncturist about this recently and he told me that energy gets stuck in midlife women.

Varying our activities is good
- When we alternate sedentary work with physically active tasks and restful periods, we can accomplish a lot each day without feeling stressed.
- Checking in with ourselves often will let us know what's needed.
- Regular rest periods allow us to be more productive.

In his book *The 20 Minute Break*, Ernest Rossi advises breaking every two hours for twenty minutes to rejuvenate ourselves. This increases our productivity significantly, so no need to feel guilty about intermixing work and breaks. The idea behind the recommendation is that our body has two-hour cycles of high and low energy.

There's a *Self-care Checklist* in the '*Exercise Booklet*'. You can use it on a daily basis, and it can be especially helpful when you're going through a difficult period.

Becoming the observer
- We function automatically much of our waking hours.
- Sometimes it's good to step back and observe ourselves.
- Take note of all the tasks we're doing each day and how we're pacing ourselves; we'll recognize when and where to introduce more balance into our day.
- Simply taking a deep breath will bring awareness into our bodies and slow down our busy minds.

When we take the time to check in with ourselves, we usually find that we know very well what makes us feel good and what nourishes us as women

- Putting our own needs first *wherever* possible will change our relationships with our loved ones dramatically because we'll feel invigorated.

Scheduling personal time just as we would any other appointment solves the problem for many women. When our own time is written in our daybook we can honestly answer that we're already committed when we're asked to take on extra tasks. *If we don't prioritize our time, it's highly unlikely that we'll get time for ourselves!*

It all depends on the decisions we're willing to make about how we use our time. The small changes we make today will become strong habits over time as we lay the foundation for an enriched life.

Balance in all things is the key in midlife – whether it's in our diet, exercise, social activities or our caregiving. When we provide balance for ourselves we will thrive, not just survive!

NOTES:

Chapter 7 - Dealing With Many Emotions as a Caregiver

We arrive at the door marked *caregiver* by many routes. Some of us were subtly groomed from an early age to be the one to take charge when our parent grew old. Others have found that they've become their parent's primary caregiver due to their life circumstances. Perhaps they are the adult child who lives nearest to the parent, or maybe they're the only daughter or daughter-in-law in the family. Some women have no sibling to help them because they're an only child, or their siblings are unable or unwilling to share in the parent's care.

Take a little time to think about how it happened that you came into the caregiving role. Understanding the underlying dynamics will help you clarify what you're doing and why you're doing it, and will provide you with a stronger basis for asking those around you for the help and support you need.

How caregiving affects us emotionally

Most families of our generation don't talk much about feelings, but when our parent is aging or ill many emotional issues arise for both the primary caregiver and for other family members. It can be a very challenging time for everyone.

My neighbor recently experienced this when her mother in New York State broke her hip in a fall. She and her siblings had very different emotional reactions to the crisis. Some were 'too busy' to help, while others implied that they couldn't cope. My neighbor was the adult child who was able and willing to take charge of the situation, flying over two thousand miles to her mother's bedside.

We're the generation caught between growing families and aging parents, with our jobs somewhere in the middle. Managing our stress while balancing these responsibilities can be a challenge.

When acting as caregivers, we spend so much time nurturing our parent it's hard to identify our own feelings. Often, we are not able to acknowledge the true emotions inside us because we don't think we have a right to them. We tell ourselves it's our duty to look after our parent, or become convinced that we must be the one to step forward because there's no one else to do it.

Feeling guilty

Guilt is one of the most persistent and debilitating feelings for a caregiver. Our guilt may be for things we think we did wrong in the past, or for our present, *perceived* inadequacies. Sometimes we feel others, such as paid caregivers and other family members, are doing more than we are for our parent. Part of me feels this way. As a well-trained, loving daughter, shouldn't I be the one looking after my mom? The curious thing is that guilt is particularly common in the most devoted adult children. I've felt my share of it over the past ten years.

In her book *"Caring For Yourself While Caring for Your Aging Parents"*, Claire Berman is very forthcoming about the many reasons she experiences guilt, for example, for finding visits to her aging mother and mother-in-law a duty, and for being healthy and leading an active life when they're not able to.

I've tried to include my mother in activities with family and friends whenever possible over the past few years so she could enjoy stimulating venues and mix with people of all ages. She attended many co-housing group events in the past, but now that she's so frail and interacts less with outsiders, it's harder for her to socialize.

Guilt takes a toll on us because it gradually wears us down and weakens us both physically and emotionally. It's hard to make good decisions or give high quality care to our parent when we feel this way.

In our heartfelt desire to give our parent the best care possible and to have a close relationship with them, sometimes we get carried away and develop impractical plans based on our dreams of an ideal life with our parent. For example some women choose, consciously or unconsciously, to live with or very near their mother or father in order to heal past issues and develop a better relationship with them, but very often the dramatic improvements they are seeking do not manifest.

Anticipating what's to come

- Women who are actively involved with their parent often experience anxiety and grief *in anticipation* of the future.

As time goes on, adult children may feel a constant subtle undercurrent of dread about what will happen next. We may feel depressed and sad as we slowly come to accept that our parent will not recover.

It took me several years to realize on a conscious level how powerfully my mother's slow downward descent affected me. Physical decline is expected in elders; her mental losses have been harder to accept. As she moved further inside herself over the years, I've had a sense of being slowly abandoned by my mother. A young part inside of me wants to cry out, "Come back". The day is coming when she may not recognize us as her family members.

When our parent goes into care

- Many adult children are afraid that having their parent move into a nursing home will be viewed as failing them or abandoning them.

My feelings about my mother and her slow deterioration have been complex. I've been able to process some of them through my dreams. After she had been in care for several years I had two dreams. In the first the authorities said they couldn't look after her anymore, that she needed to be 'warehoused', and that I should take her to my home. In the next dream the same people put her in the 'back ward' of a care facility, (i.e. a place for hopelessly ill people).

In reality, my mother has been happy in her two care homes for close to five years. She was very lonely during her thirty years as a widow. She's a very outgoing person and loves being around others.

- Knowing when a parent is 'ready for care' is not an easy question to answer.

Some professionals say the elder is never ready, it's up to the caregiver to decide. That's certainly the case with some families, but it didn't happen that way with us. Our doctor said our mother was 'borderline safe' in her own apartment and that many people stay at home too long. Even with her worsening dementia, Mom understood that her living situation was deteriorating. She agreed that she couldn't go on as she was in her apartment, even with daily help. I told her I would find a good place for her in North Vancouver near us and she said she would try it out.

- I personally believe the decision to move into care should ultimately be the parent's, *unless they can't participate in making a proper decision.*
- Today's elder care philosophy maintains that seniors must be allowed to choose to live at risk as long as they are cognitively able to make decisions and understand the risks involved.

Getting professional advice gives us accurate information and helps take some of the burden of guilt from our shoulders. The opinion of a professional can help us to manage our strong emotions about our parent's care. Then we can be clearer in our thinking when we make decisions. There is a fine line in this process between our parent's expressed desire, our opinion, and the advice of professionals.

The care home's responsibility versus ours – "Who's in control?"

When my mom went into care I knew the decision we'd made together was right for her, but I approached the move with a mixture of strong feelings. I felt sad about what had happened to her mind, and was helpless to stop her decline. I tried my best to make everything just right for her in her new surroundings. Her bedside table was arranged nicely with an embroidered cloth, one of her own lamps and a tape player with her Welsh music, and I always kept fresh flowers in her room.

But it just wasn't possible to maintain this hoped for standard because I wasn't the one in charge of my mother's care, and had little control over her daily situation in reality. It saddened me when her plants died because they weren't watered, or her belongings disappeared. I slowly let go of my attempt to give her a perfect life; it was too stressful for me, and in the end it didn't really make a difference to her overall well-being. It was the legal responsibility of the care home and its staff to look after her, and I realized I had to let them do the job they were trained for and dedicated to.

- Our parent must have an advocate when they're in care.

A good care facility welcomes input from family, involves the residents in decision-making, and responds in a real way to the concerns of both. The staff understand that the care of our parents may be an emotional issue.

I resolved a potentially serious overmedication problem early on by working closely with the nursing co-ordinator and engaging an excellent doctor who did not believe in unnecessary meds. The staff grew to understand and to love my mother over time, and things progressed very well.

Loving in a new way
- Our complicated feelings about our parent's decline may lead us to over function as caregivers.
- Trying to do too much to compensate is a common pitfall.

Moving to a care facility means a step closer to complete dependence, and finally death. In retrospect, I believe my desire to make my mother's surroundings 'just right' was an attempt to control her downward spiral and make her life seem more normal. Since my mom could no longer look after herself at home, I wanted her to be well cared for and surrounded by beauty so her quality of life was as high as possible.

- Unrealistic expectations of ourselves and our parent can make us feel frustrated with them.

Sometimes adult children get frustrated with their parent's behavior, their attitude, or their forgetfulness. My aunt used to correct her mother-in-law (my maternal grandmother) each time she forgot something or became confused because of her dementia. Naturally this didn't help her mother-in-law's condition at all. (Ironically my aunt developed severe Alzheimer's herself in later years.)

Our biggest challenge is to accept that our parent's abilities are waning. We experience loss too when they become physically handicapped, lose their sight or hearing, or become mentally impaired. It's been an ongoing process for me to grasp the full implications of my mother's situation. My own mortality has been brought home to me also as I watch my parent slowly decline.

We go through similar stages when our parents age as when they die.
- At first we can't believe what's happening.
- Later we may feel angry or sad that it's so soon.
- Then we may bargain in an attempt to delay their decline (e.g. if I do this for her; or if she stops that, etc.).
- Finally, we adjust to varying degrees to what has upset us, and learn to live with the situation.

Humans really are resilient. I'm surprised at how well I and my family have adjusted our thinking and our feelings as our mother has slowly declined. The new relationship that has emerged for my mother and me has a bittersweet flavor. Although I am very saddened by her loss of faculties, the new closeness that has emerged with our unconditional acceptance of each other is very heartwarming.

When we begin to reverse the roles we've always had with our parent, a lifelong relationship is profoundly altered. The parent we knew is no longer there for us though they are alive. My 'little mommy' dreams were my mind's way of sorting out the role reversal from child-daughter to 'pillar of strength' for my mother. If we're able to actively deal with our painful feelings, we'll feel better about our changing relationship with our parents.

The most important thing is that we ensure a quality of care for our parent that meets our needs too. Then we can counsel ourselves to let go, and forgive ourselves for whatever is over and done with. That's really all we need to do.

NOTES:

Chapter 8 - Asking for Help

Superwoman

Women find it hard to face the reality of a twenty-four hour day. We continue to overextend ourselves by striving to be everything to everyone. This is especially true when it comes to looking after our elderly parents. Some of us immerse ourselves totally in our caregiving, with little attention paid to the other parts of our lives.

Claire Berman, author of *"Caring For Yourself While Caring For Your Aging Parents"*, calls these adult children 'super caregivers'. She says:

> "Many super caregivers are so attuned to the needs of their parent and dedicated to meeting them that they lose sight of their own lives, their own requirements, and become depressed, distressed and drained." [5]

Although I have never been a full time caregiver for my mother, I relate to the idea of being highly attuned to the needs of my parent. I tried to ensure that none of her needs went unmet and also to make a heart-to-heart connection with her. It's good to come together in this way, but if we effort too much I believe our endeavors can become a bit obsessive.

We don't like to admit we need help

Many of us presuppose that we must look after the lion's share of our parent's care for a number of reasons.

1. We've been conditioned to look after others by our upbringing.
2. New brain research shows women's biology fosters a built-in desire to nurture.
3. We may not have the funds for paid caregivers.
4. We love our parent and want to spend time with them.
5. We have a desire to heal past issues.
6. Communication issues with siblings and other family may preclude asking for the necessary help.
7. We pride ourselves on our ability to succeed in every area.

It's often hard for strong, competent women to reach out. We're so used to relying on ourselves to do it all we forget that we have limits. Sometimes we make excuses for maintaining the status quo. We may even pay caregivers to help, but still micro-manage their work.

---

[5] Reprinted by permission of the author.

Do you hear yourself saying any of these things?
- "I always cope, I don't need anyone."
- "Everyone else is too busy."
- "They won't do it right."
- "It'll be quicker if I do it myself."

These thoughts can be so embedded in our minds we're not always conscious of them. Consequently we often become increasingly tired, irritable and perhaps even slightly resentful over time.

A team approach

Although we're all highly capable, we do need others to help carry the load. A team approach benefits all concerned. Let's step outside ourselves for a moment and stretch our thinking. Getting others involved in our parent's care is not just about meeting our needs as caregivers. Not only does it spare us some of our emotional and physical stress, it also enriches our parent's life.

Our team care plan can include anything we want it to - from full care for our parent, to a specific amount of paid assistance for housework and companionship, to volunteer help, to a professional care manager if we live far away. (Note: Paid help may be a combination of private and government funding).

- A team approach lightens the emotional and physical load.
- Our parent's life is fuller and more stimulating with more people involved in it.
- It's rewarding for all those involved.

Before my mother went into care she enjoyed having several women spend time with her in her home and do light chores for her. In the care home she has welcomed the attention of the kindly care aides and nurses.

I can't emphasize enough the importance of making the effort to build good relationships with our parent's professional support team. These are the doctors, nurses, care aides and therapists… the ones who look after our parent each and every day. When they get to know us as individuals and see us with our parent, they'll take the extra steps needed to remedy any problem that may arise, and ensure we're given updates on our parent. This will give us peace of mind and the confidence that they're well cared for.

We're fortunate that the same dedicated doctor we all had before leaving the Sunshine Coast agreed to be our doctor again when we returned. At my mother's first care conference here the staff remarked to Dr. Ron that he was the only doctor who attended the patient conferences.

How to reach out to family members

Family relationships are often complex, therefore many of us hesitate to ask for assistance. Primary caregivers may believe that close relatives already know what help is needed, or make the assumption that they won't respond.

From the other point of view, family members may be used to one person taking charge and getting things done, and they may be quite comfortable with the status quo. They may even resent being asked to take on a greater role.

If we first clarify for ourselves what we as primary caregiver are able to do, it will be much easier to discuss the situation with other family members. Take the time to write an itemized outline of the current caregiving situation including:
- Your parent's needs
- The tasks you are performing
- What still requires attention

We can then make suggestions to help family members know what's needed. For instance,
- Siblings and other members of the family who don't do hands-on work may be able and willing to provide money for care.
- Some family members are good at tasks like financial management, or acting as a liaison with care facility administration, government, medical staff or lawyers.
- On the days you're with your parent, let your partner and children know how they can help out with simple tasks like doing laundry, starting dinner or washing dishes.

Think outside the box

If getting help from family, friends and neighbors doesn't work out, think of *alternative support systems*. With some networking, some sleuthing and lots of perseverance it's possible to find people to visit your elder and do many practical tasks for them, either on a volunteer basis or for a nominal fee.

- Churches and high schools are good resources for finding caregivers and visitors.
- Some churches have rosters of volunteers willing to visit elderly people.
- Many youth do volunteer work or make paid visits to the elderly as part of community outreach and course credit.

- Friends and neighbors sometimes visit each other's parents who live in the same home, just as they once shared childcare.
- Most communities have volunteer associations set up.

When we enlist the help of others they won't do things exactly the way we do them ourselves. But stop for a moment and ask yourself: "Does it really matter?". Perhaps letting go of our high standard for our parent's care might be a positive thing. It could be an important part of us taking responsibility for our own self-care. I found letting go helped me put things in perspective.

Others interact with our parent and do the necessary tasks in their own way, which in most cases will be just fine. The bottom line is, as long as we feel comfortable with the helper and assured of their trustworthiness, we need not micro-manage what they're doing.

How to make it work

Eckhart Tolle says we take ourselves very seriously when we play roles. I believe this is particularly true for the parts we play as adults. We often forget to be spontaneous and joyful. Sometimes we immerse ourselves deeply in our roles and they become a large part of who we are.

Most of us find many of our activities very fulfilling. I personally find connecting with my clients, caring for my mother and writing all strike deep emotional, psychological and spiritual chords within me. However, I still need plenty of time for other, non-structured activities like reading, gardening and just relaxing, to find balance.

It's time for us to step outside the constraints of our caregiver roles. Let's experiment and find out what works best for us. When we're happy and energetic, that affects how our parent and other family members feel. When we're burned out we and our parent are both deprived of the joy of each other's company.

The operative word when it comes to our parent's care may be compromise. By doing this we can produce a win-win situation that satisfies us and keeps them happy and safe. For example, lately I've used the Handy Dart bus service to bring my mother to my home to visit and enjoy the garden. Initially part of me felt as a good daughter I should drive my mother myself (two hours driving for me). But she enjoyed the road trip with her attentive driver, and met people she knew on the way home. Now after three successful visits, I accept this mutually satisfactory arrangement.

- Take a leaf from my book, and even if you're not totally at ease with your 'out of the box behavior' yet, *act as if you are.*

- You will become comfortable enough with it soon.

Change doesn't have to come all at once. With small but consistent *'turtle steps'* we can make healthy transitions for both ourselves and our parent.

NOTES:

Chapter 9 - Your Spiritual Connection

When we are caregivers our spiritual expression can support us in many ways. It can soften and deepen our relationship with our parent and help us to accept their limitations. It offers a way for us to *thrive* throughout the experience of caregiving, rather than simply to *survive* it.

Having a sense of the spiritual allows us:
- To refresh and renew ourselves on an ongoing basis.
- To step outside our daily '*doing*' and go to a quieter place.

Whether we're taking a few moments for a walk or practicing breathing deeply we'll sense our spiritual connection. It can also be found when we are formally meditating or attending a religious service.

The idea that we are a synthesis of body, mind *and* spirit is more readily accepted now in our western culture. We realize we need more than just a body and a mind to take us through our day. Self-help books and magazines often talk about how our spirit requires attention and feeding, but do we really know how to look after our own spiritual well being?

It's important to remember that spirituality is very individual; what fulfills us spiritually is unique to each of us. We need to take some time to discover what carries us outside of our usual way of being in the world – away from our thinking, our emotions, and our daily concerns - to a place where we feel more at peace.

A satisfying sense of spirituality is one that weaves itself through our days in small ways. When I took a Buddhist workshop last spring, the teacher told us they think westerners are funny because we believe we have to sit for hours meditating formally. (In fact, this is how I was taught to do my Kriya Yoga meditation in 2001). However, the Buddhist instructor says, just take your cup of coffee, go outside, sit down, take a breath and meditate for five minutes. This is better than not doing it at all.

I feel that as individuals we often approach our body, our mind, and our spirit as if they are disconnected from each other. It's the tendency of our culture to compartmentalize, for example, look at the way our medicine treats various organs and body parts separately when they're actually interrelated. Therefore, it is natural that we often view our body, mind and spirit as separate rather than as a whole as some cultures do.

- We don't always recognize that we bring the whole of us to everything we do, whether it be our work, a walk in the woods, or time with our parent.

- We enrich ourselves when we do what nurtures us spiritually, such as meditation, prayer or gardening.
- When we remember that our body, mind and spirit are inseparable we can be mindful about our complete well-being everywhere we go.

What does feeding our spirit mean?

Spiritual expression can take many forms, from the religious and formal to the more informal *'new age'* practices that can include nature, the body, sexuality, movement, relationships, art and music.

My own definition of spirituality is very broad and embraces a range of beliefs, from the existence of a Higher Power I'm comfortable naming *'God'* or *'Goddess'*, to a deep appreciation of the mysteries of nature. Ultimately I believe *anything that adds positive meaning to our life is spiritual.*

Walking in the woods, spending time with a child, gardening or making love with our partner is a spiritual expression for many women. For others, meditation, mountain climbing or a career of service gives meaning.

Some women find a form of strength and comfort through returning to church, synagogue, or some other place that offers religious or spiritual support. A group practice creates a positive, healing energy for many of us. As a young child I was brought up in the Welsh United Church in Toronto, a small church that fit the Welsh stereotype of roof-shaking singing. Several years ago I sang in the choir of the local United Church for about two years, and it suited my spiritual needs at that time.

A broader definition of spirituality can provide sustenance for many women, especially for those of us who choose not to practice formal religion. My eclectic blend of beliefs suits me and is very comforting.

Getting lost in our daily living
- Sometimes we become caught up in lives that deplete us rather than serving our needs.

When the practical tasks of daily living take on an out-of-proportion significance, we lose our connection with the gentle, joyful part of ourselves. When we step outside our routines even briefly, we get a sense of something different. This shift from the *doing* of tasks to a quieter place of *being* can happen in many different ways and in any setting we find ourselves in.

Some possible ways to make this shift are:
- Walking while focusing all our senses on our surroundings.
- Pausing periodically during our workday to take a deep breath in and out.
- Listening for and following the guidance of our intuition or gut feeling.

Creating stillness

Many of us breath quite shallowly, especially when we're feeling rushed and tense. When I was a Trager bodyworker I noticed that often when women lay on the massage table the rise and fall of their diaphragm was barely noticeable.

Shallow breathing is a habit developed over time. It can easily be unlearned with body awareness and repetition.
- Use post-its to help you remind yourself to tune in to your breathing regularly.
- Many clients find this simple breathing exercises helpful:
    - Inhale deeply, hold your breath for 2-5 seconds, then exhale vigorously.
    - This will oxygenate your body and lower your stress level.

Eckhart Tolle says breathing is key to our all round well-being. Taking deep breaths connects us with the still place where our spirit lives. We cannot think our thoughts when we're concentrating on our breathing, and we create a still space for ourselves.

> "In the silence between the beats of the music we find stillness." [6]
> Zeta Gaudet

My Pure Motion dance instructor also speaks of stillness when she draws our attention to the pauses between the notes of the music. In this space we stop and rest for a brief moment. We twirl and spiral, making movements in the same shape as the DNA in our body. I feel pure, childlike bliss as I turn, and I leave the class with a feeling of overall well-being. It's as if my physical body has reconnected with my spiritual body.

When we are overworked as caregivers, it's easy to leave the stillness behind. We can counteract this by paying careful attention to what's going on inside us. Then, as we go through the day we can do small things to feed our spirit. This pays off exponentially.

Use memory aids as a reminder to give yourself small rewards that will enrich you. Build the following into each day:
- Go outside for some fresh air.

---

[6] Reprinted by permission of the author.

- Connect with a positive person like a friend or coworker.
- Close your eyes and take a few deep breaths to soothe and calm yourself.

Our bodies offer us a great gift… the gift of information. The body never lies – its tension lets us know when we're stressed. When we teach ourselves to check in frequently, we will be able to read our emotions, our thoughts and our spiritual state easily. Then we'll know what we need and how to respond. This ultimately enables us to balance ourselves during all activities.

Aging as a spiritual experience

Being a caregiver for our elderly parent can be a very moving, spiritual experience. When we connect with each other deeply, something happens that goes beyond ordinary day-to-day communication.

I always benefit from my visits with my mother. We relate in a way that words can't capture… through our eyes and through the tranquil mood between us. We have a special relationship and our time together nurtures both of us.

The atmosphere in my mother's home is relaxed and nurturing. The staff pride themselves on their highly skilled, personal, loving care. Those who work in care homes fulfill a very special role by caring for elders who are in *'end of life care'*. There is a quality of gentle compassion in the seasoned nurses and care aides I've had the honor to meet. A care aide recently told me that she is in the business of helping people pass over. I found it very hopeful that she added this spiritual dimension to the process unfolding by naming it as such.

Whether or not we are able to have a close emotional and spiritual connection with our parent, it's important that we find ways to feed our own spirit at this time. When we do this consistently we feel a lightness within.

Midlife is a time when most of us are naturally searching both consciously and unconsciously for ways to feel more aligned with our true selves. This process is facilitated by peace, quietness, and time alone. As we care for ourselves spiritually we create a domino effect that gives permission to everyone around us to do the same.

- I invite you to choose experiences that resonate deep within you - in your heart and your spirit - and give yourself the gift of them often.
- Keep checking in with yourself, and with a little practice, you will get clear answers.
- Honor these answers as much as possible.
- It is your right to celebrate your spirituality.

Chapter 10 - Putting it all together

Choosing how we want to live

When we don't live in a mindful way, we're acting from a default position. The dictionary definition of default is "A failure to act". In computer language it means "A course of action that a program will take when the *user specifies no overriding action*". I like this definition because I feel it applies to the situations women find themselves in. If we don't take action towards what we want, it just won't happen.

How might we apply this metaphor to our lives? Sometimes when it comes to our personal life we go along with what's asked of us, not being proactive about the direction that takes us in. Maybe we're fulfilling the expectations of others… perhaps it feels easier not to make waves, to just go with the flow.

Choosing how we want to live means recognizing that we have limitations, and knowing just what they are. Then we're able to set our own clear priorities, deciding how much we're able to do and how much we truly want to do. We can bring other individuals and services on board as needed, and include other family members in our parent's care wherever possible. This way everyone has an investment in the care of our elder, and we're all able to share the good times with them.

Sharing the caring

We feel alone in our role of caregiver, especially when others don't seem to realize the impact being a caregiver has on our lives. Unfortunately as human beings we don't always relate to what other people are living through unless we experience something similar.

My fellow coach, Bridgette Boudreau, recently shared on her blog a clever idea for getting others to understand our work overwhelm. The article describes a businesswoman's plan to get her boss to share the stress of her workload. In brief, the idea was to invite her boss to choose which of her numerous projects should be done first. In this way the supervisor would become engaged in problem solving and share some of the stress involved in the heavy workload. Hence their understanding of the situation would grow.

I believe we can adapt this idea to our personal lives, to help us bring family members and friends on board with the idea of sharing the caregiving. There are many advantages to letting others know what needs to be done and getting their opinion on how issues should be approached. We get fresh outside input when we do this. When the whole family shares in the decision making and the work allotment, some of the primary caregiver load is lifted.

- Regular phone calls with our siblings help keep everyone 'on the same page'.
- When the whole family is up to speed about the elder's life they feel more involved and are therefore more likely to be helpful.
- Sometimes being asked to do small tasks will encourage family members who are reluctant to help.
- Adult children may not visit often, but may agree to make regular check-in calls to their father or mother.
- Brothers and sisters who are short of time or don't feel close to their parent may, if asked, contribute the funds to cover expenses.

Managing the caregiving

Sometimes our parent may want us to visit immediately or want things done right away. Perhaps we feel we *must* visit because it's our appointed day. But as time goes on we realize that there's usually no urgency to get things done, in fact some tasks aren't even necessary. We begin to relax into the process more and start to pace ourselves.

We learn to assess and prioritize the requests:
- Brief, planned phone calls will help our aging parent feel more secure.
- Minor problems can often be solved by phone, without waiting for an in-person visit.
- Often what our parent needs is reassurance that we'll always be in their life.

A daughter quoted in Claire Berman's book says:

> "I'll always be there for my mother when she needs me, but I don't think I do either one of us a favor by being at her beck and call." [7]

I agree with this. We need other aspects to our life in addition to our relationship with our parent. My mother understood and accepted this. One day some time ago, she noticed concern on my face when I was leaving her, and realized it was hard for me to go. She looked at me, and said in a strong voice: "I'm *fine* Ellen".

Part of knowing our limits is ensuring that the choices we make are for the right reasons. If much of our caregiving comes from guilt, obligation or duty, our energy will be sapped and our pleasure in the time with our parent will diminish. When we're clear about our part in the relationship we will both benefit.

---

[7] Reprinted by permission of the author.

- Take an honest look at everything you do for your parent.
- Ask yourself what the purpose behind each choice is.
- If any of your activities are:
  - Unnecessary
  - Unpleasant for you
  - Performed only out of duty
  - Done out of guilt

Consider eliminating them or passing them on to others.

Being a caregiver is an important part of our life, but it's not necessary or healthy to let it consume us. Claire Berman says:

> "Sometimes there's a fine line between dedication and martyrdom, between selflessness and self-preservation when it comes to caregiving." [8]

It's the task of each of us to define this line and to find the place of balance that works best for all.

Simplifying our lives

We can pare down and simplify all aspects of our lives so our activities benefit rather than drain us. With care we can plan our schedules, including our caregiving, so it all works *for us* rather than *against us*. When we do this our days have a flow… a rhythm to them that nurtures and comforts us.

- Begin your day slowly, to set the tone for the whole day.
- Find a morning ritual that works for you:
  - Breathing exercises, meditation or stretching
  - Coffee in bed or breakfast on the back porch.
  - Going for a brisk walk
- Take five to ten minutes at intervals throughout the day to relax and breathe slowly.
- When you'd rather not do something, give yourself the option of: [9]
  - Doing it for a shorter time
  - Doing it less often
  - Not doing it all

---

[8] Reprinted by permission of the author.

[9] This tip adapted from Martha Beck's work.

These simple things make a profound difference to our day… the difference between struggle and ease.

Once we're able to give ourselves permission, we can set suitable boundaries and seek help from others. We can now choose to live proactively instead of by default. When we develop a workable plan for what we're able to do and not do as caregivers and as women, we experience richness in our lives. We live a life of balance.

A New Way of Living

> "As you think thoughts that feel good, you will be in harmony with *who-you-really-are*. And in doing so you will utilize your profound freedom. *Seek joy first, and all of the growth that you could ever imagine will come joyously and abundantly unto you.*" [10]
> Abraham-Hicks

Women in midlife are now on a journey to reclaim ourselves, to assert our right to be the best woman we can possibly be. We're taking actions that reflect this priority and breaking away from some of the old, limiting roles and stereotypes that linger on.

It takes bravery to create an authentic life… to step out into the world, to speak our mind, to buck the system. We are the generation that took all the risks, often without even realizing or being acknowledged for it. We're powerful, talented women and we shine in the face of challenges.

To develop a new way of living is a gradual process. As we set renewed priorities and question automatic reactions that lead us to rush in wherever help is needed, our old ways are replaced with an intentional approach, one that includes living our own best lives while also taking into account our interdependence with others.

As our aging population grows and we become more vocal about what's needed for elder care, society will alter its thinking, attitudes and beliefs, and consequently awareness will increase significantly. With time the invisible work of caregiving will be valued and honored, our stories will be told, and appropriate government services and funding will become available.

Major cultural differences exist around the world towards aging and death. In western society we try to defy them, but some cultures accept the transition more readily and believe that the spirits of the dead live amongst us. A continuity and connectedness are implicit in their visits to the graves of loved ones. These customs make it easier to accept death and decline than our culture's do.

The courage we call forth as we redefine our lives does not come free of fear and self doubt. I experience both regularly as I stretch myself professionally and personally, risking in all areas, especially emotionally. Even those of us who are very accomplished still feel the fear that originates in the old reptilian part of our brain. Yet when we keep moving forward, turtle step by turtle step, our comfort grows day by day as we transform ourselves anew.

---

[10] Jerry & Esther Hicks, Daily Quotes, Summer 2008, www.abraham-hicks.com

Through it all, allow yourself to dream. From our dreams come our visions. When we develop a strong internal vision - one so compelling we can't help but take action on it – this vision helps us move through our fears and setbacks and keeps us moving ahead into our new way of living.

We'll experience a growing sense of sureness as we continue to follow the emerging path towards our new future. It may be very subtle, and likely transitory, but over time the feeling of joy and freedom will grow. A deep knowing will be awakened in us… a recognition that we are living our lives as we are meant to…in a way that allows us to share our unique gifts with the world.

Thank you for letting me take this journey with you.

Ellen Besso, MidLife woman, mother, and daughter

Exercise Booklet

Surviving Eldercare: Where Their Needs End and Yours Begin

by Ellen Besso

The exercise booklet and any of the exercises accompanying Surviving Eldercare are not meant to take the place of professional therapy

Chapter 1 - Who Are You?

My Life as a Caregiver

Briefly name 3 parts of your life that you're most proud of:

_____
_____
_____
_____
_____

Note the type of tasks you do for the person you care for and the number of hours spent at each:

Category	Hours per month
Personal Care	_____
Appointments	_____
Social Time	_____
Shopping	_____
Management	_____
Other Tasks	_____
Other Tasks	_____
Other Tasks	_____

List the 3 most important things you do in your caregiving:

_____
_____
_____
_____

Do you think you're a typical caregiver?

_____
_____
_____
_____

Chapter 2 - Trying to Do Too Much

Caregiver Self-assessment

There are many signs that tell us whether we've become too stressed by our caregiving duties.

Check off the ones that apply to you:

- ☐ I feel anxious a lot of the time
- ☐ Sometimes I resent my parent or other family members
- ☐ I'm not enjoying my hobbies and socializing anymore
- ☐ I'm tired all the time but can't get to sleep or oversleep sometimes
- ☐ I seem to get every virus going around
- ☐ I'm much more irritable than before
- ☐ I've lost or gained a lot of weight lately
- ☐ My exercise regime has gone out the window
- ☐ I often have headaches or stomach aches

Pruning Your Caregiving Tasks

For this exercise you'll need your list of categories from *Chapter 1, My Tasks as a Caregiver Exercise*.

1. Take a couple of deep breaths in, then out.
2. Break each category down into a list of specific tasks.

    Example: *Appointments: dental, eye, specialist*

3. Without self-monitoring, quickly mark an X beside the items on your list that:

    - You'd really rather not do
    - You realize aren't really necessary
    - You can put off doing for a time
    - Someone else can do just as well

Now you're prepared for the next part of this process: ***eliminating*** some of your tasks.

1. Right now cross the unnecessary items off your list.
2. Plan how to get the rest done by:
    a. Re-scheduling the tasks that can be delayed

    Example: *clothes shopping*

    b. Making a list of tasks others can do (include how often and number of hours)

    Examples: a *volunteer will visit parent twice a month*

3. Each week divest yourself of 2 items from the above list.
4. Be sure to ask your friends and family for ideas.

Taking tiny, incremental steps will make your change comfortable. Think of this as a commitment to ***you.***

Chapter 3 - How We Change in MidLife

Assessing My Midlife Changes

How is my life better now?

_____
_____
_____

Examples: *I feel more sense of connection with spirit & self.*
I worry less about pleasing others.

What needs to change for my life to improve even more?

_____
_____
_____

Example: *I need some extra time to concentrate on my health.*
I'd like to work fewer hours at both paid and unpaid tasks.

What is the limiting thought that keeps me from moving forward with this?

_____
_____
_____

Examples: *There's not enough time.*
My monthly expenses are too high.

I challenge you to make a decision to change one limiting thought or behavior today!

NOTES:

Chapter 4 – How Our Relationships Change

Changes in My Relationships

Close your eyes, take a deep breath then slowly exhale.
List 3 relationships in your life and note one way each has changed.

Relationship   The Change

_____   _____

_____   _____

_____   _____

My Relationship With My Parent

What are 3 good things about your relationship with your parent?

_____

_____

_____

Examples: *We laugh together sometimes.*
            I can't think of anything good right now.

What do you believe your parent needs from you the most?

_____

_____

_____

Examples: *Love*
            Regular visits
            Supervision of their care

Caregiver Stress

The feelings that cause me stress as a caregiver are:

_____
_____
_____
_____

The stressful thought behind each feeling is:

_____
_____
_____
_____

This is the way I behave or the action I take:

_____
_____
_____
_____

Examples: (Feeling) *I worry if I take a vacation,*
(Thought) *my parent may be lonely or neglected,*
(Behavior) *so I'll only take a weekend off.*

(Feeling) *I feel guilty if someone else takes my parent to the dentist,*
(Thought) *I'm a bad daughter,*
(Behavior) *so I always take her myself*

Chapter 5 - Thoughts That Run the Show

Breathing - Our First Line of Defense

Breathing is our most important tool for stress reduction and it's so simple.

- It gets us out of our heads
- It lowers our stress level

Inhale deeply through your nose; hold as long as it's comfortable; exhale forcefully through your mouth.

- If you do this 3-5 times every 15-30 minutes, you'll feel vibrant and relaxed.
    - If you can't do the full exercise, single breaths are also effective.
    - Use this any time to relax, and before changing tasks.

Let's Stop the Racing

- Go to a place you're familiar with.
- Take a couple of deep breaths, and then continue breathing comfortably.
- Walk around, and as you walk, just notice everything around you.
- Using each of your senses in turn, note 3 things in your surroundings.
  Note: This activity works best outside.

Dealing With Unwanted Thoughts

2 exercise options:

1. **Thought Stopping**
   - This is a way to stop dwelling on a thought that won't leave you alone.
   - Monitor yourself, and when you catch yourself thinking the thought, simply raise your hand and say out loud ***Stop!*** (If you're around others, do it in silently).
   - Once you've done this for awhile, you'll simply need to think 'Stop' to get results.

2. *Thought Embracing*

- If you find a negative or stressful thought is persisting, simply notice it without judging yourself for it.
- Write your thought down when it occurs so you'll begin to notice when and where it happens.

Mentally embrace your thought as a valid part of who you are.

Chapter 6 - Taking Care of You

Relaxation Body Scan
- Sit in a quiet place.
- Begin with your 3-5 breath exercise (from '*Thoughts*' chapter).
- Starting at the top of your head, slowly move your focus downward, noticing how your body feels.
- Each time you locate a spot that's tight, sore or bothers you in any way (including emotionally), just breathe into it.
- Imagine healing energy is going into this area (colored or white light).
- Daily practice of this exercise will help you notice your body more and relax the tension in it.

The Gift of Time
- Take a deep breath. Now imagine putting yourself first on your schedule, just like paying yourself first when you put savings in the bank. Now fill in the following:

If I was first on my schedule I would:

_____
_____
_____

Examples: *Give myself a mini-holiday each week (massage or other self-care).*
Learn something new I've always wanted to do.

Specific actions to put yourself first:

_____
_____
_____

Examples: *I will arrange for 2 hours of alone time each weekend.*
I will make an appointment to begin piano lessons.

Self-care Checklist

- ☐ I eat 3-5 high quality meals & snacks each day
- ☐ I drink plenty of water
- ☐ My caffeine & alcohol intake is moderate
- ☐ I do some kind of exercise each day
- ☐ I take 3-5 deep breaths every 15-30 minutes
- ☐ I go outside in the fresh air daily
- ☐ I get 7-9 hours sleep per night
- ☐ I ensure I take some time alone each day
- ☐ I check in with my support system regularly
- ☐ During the day I vary my tasks & take mini breaks often

Other things I do to feed myself are:

_____

_____

_____

Chapter 7 - Dealing With Many Emotions as a Caregiver

Practical Ways to Deal With Our Emotions
List some bothersome emotions, then some practical ways to shift them:

Emotion	Helpful Action
_____	_____
_____	_____
_____	_____

Examples:
Overwhelmed   *Take a mental health day from all work.*
                        Book a lunch date with a friend.

Allover tension   *Stretch every morning & during the day.*

Dealing With Strong Feelings as a Caregiver

Guilt:

What I feel guilty about	How I can change the situation
_____	_____
_____	_____
_____	_____

Examples:
My parent is alone far away   *I can hire a local case manager*
I don't take my parent out enough   *I'll make 1 extra visit every 2 weeks*

Anger :
Often we stuff our anger with addictive behaviors.[11] Do you do any of the following?

- ☐ Overeat at meals
- ☐ Gorge on chocolate or snacks
- ☐ Use sex often to escape
- ☐ Drink when feeling emotional
- ☐ Shop too much
- ☐ Gamble recklessly

---

[11] Seek professional help if you find your strong feelings or addictive behaviors are hard to manage.

What I feel angry about	The solution that works for me
_____	_____
_____	_____
_____	_____

My Sadness

Sometimes we hide our sadness by acting in the opposite way.
    List some ways you might be doing this.

_____   _____

_____   _____

_____   _____

Examples:
I withdraw   *I try to be upbeat at all times*
I never cry   *I tell myself 'I have to be strong'*

To release your sadness:
- Breathe deeply in and out several times.
- Invite your sadness to move through you, allow yourself to let it go. Follow what your intuition suggests to help yourself release it, e.g. journal, cry.
- For any remaining sadness use the following exercise:
    - Take 1 or 2 deep breaths, and then picture any type of container with a lid.
    - Imagine you're putting all your sadness into the container, putting the lid on and tying it up.
    - Place the container somewhere out of your sight and thoughts.

Feeding Yourself Emotionally

Make a list of what helps you to feel good and to keep positive

_____   _____

_____   _____

_____   _____

Examples:
Dance class   *Walking in nature*

Write them into your schedule and commit to doing them regularly.

Chapter 8 - Asking for Help

Why I Don't Ask For Help

I don't ask for help because:

_____

_____

_____

Example: *There's no one to help.*
           I'm not sure what's needed.

If I ask for help others will think

_____

_____

_____

Example: *I'm a bad daughter.*
           I'm not a capable person.

My Team Plan

The areas my parent needs help in are:

_____

_____

_____

When I am ready to bring others on board, those who can help are:

_____

_____

_____

Example: *My friend Mary will visit my mother.*
A private agency will supply in-home help.

Schedule for finding and asking others for help:

Task	Plan	Deadline
_____	_____	_____
_____	_____	_____
_____	_____	_____
_____	_____	_____
_____	_____	_____

Examples:
Extra visits	*Friend will visit 1X/week*	*By Jan. 31st*
Need meal prep	*Home Support 3X/week*	*By Jan. 1st*

Chapter 9 - Your Spiritual Connection

Integrating Our Body, Our Mind and Our Spirit

- Breathe deeply in and out several times.
- Begin to move your body very gently while breathing comfortably.
- Notice how your breath and the movements of your body connect.

    Example: *Sway gently from side to side.*

- Raise your arms above your head and circle them.
- Gently roll your shoulders back.

Building Spirituality Into Your Day

List 5 pastimes that nourish you spiritually and give your life meaning. In the second column, make a time commitment to yourself to enjoy this activity.

Pastime   My Commitment

_____   _____
_____   _____
_____   _____
_____   _____
_____   _____

Examples:
Breathing exercise   *Every 15 minutes*
Time alone   *30 minutes per day*
Walking in nature   *20 minutes per day*
Coffee with friends   *Once per week*

Embracing The Pauses

Option 1:

- Take a deep breath then exhale.
- Notice how you feel inside.

- Let yourself soak in the stillness.

Option 2:
- Listen to some of your favorite music.
- Notice the pauses between the notes.
- What feeling does the music generate in you?

Guidelines for Simple Living
- Begin your day slowly.
- Ignore your e-mail and phones for 3 designated periods each day.
- Recharge throughout the day with food, water and physical activity.
- Walk for 30-minutes with no goal, simply noticing what's around you.
- Practice spending unscheduled time with yourself each day (begin with 5 minutes).
- Create a relaxing atmosphere at home by lighting candles and playing soft music.
- Hug or call those who are dear to you regularly.
- Pray or meditate to seek help from a higher source.
- Offer five gratitudes each day, verbally or in writing: morning, evening and/or mid-day.

A New Way of Living

Who Inspires You?

List 2 or 3 people you admire, either real or fictional. Beside their names write down the qualities that move you.

Name	Quality
_____	_____
_____	_____
_____	_____

Our Dreams and Visions

It is important that you do your Breathing Exercises (Chapter 5) before you begin because they take you out of your head and into a more creative part of yourself.

- Take a deep breath in, hold as long as it's comfortable, then exhale hard and long.
- Repeat for 3 to 5 repetitions.

What are your deams and visions for your future? Write down 2 or 3 things that you want to do in your life:

_____
_____
_____
_____

Examples: *Start a new hobby or business*
Volunteer abroad or locally
Live beside the sea

Some Caregiving Resources for You

Books available through Amazon:
- *Caring for Yourself While Caring for Your Aging Parents*, by Claire Berman
- *14 Friends Guide to Eldercaring*
- *The Complete Eldercare Planner*, 2nd Edition by Joy Loverde

Articles & Movie:
- Jill Crossland's helpful and stimulating ezine http://timefindersmagazine.com/selffamily/relationships
- The movie *Shirley Valentine* can be purchased through http://www.Amazon.com

Web based info:
- The Caregiver Resource Center - Key issues related to planning for the future with your parents http://www.caregiverresourcecenter.com/
- Jane Gross - The New Old Age Blog http://newoldage.blogs.nytimes.com
- Amy Jeanroy - An excellent caregivers blog http://www.genbetween.com

MidLife Health Care:
- Menopause Health Information Organization – Information about all aspects of perimenopause and menopause http://menopause.health-info.org/
- Susun Weed – Articles and information about a natural approach to perimenopause http://www.susunweed.com/
- Medical Doctors, Naturopathic Doctors, qualified herbalists and Health Food stores can be found on-line or in your local yellow pages.

Dedication

Glenys and Ellen

This book is dedicated to all the caregivers, unpaid and paid, who give their time, their heart, and their soul to the care of our loved ones.

It is also dedicated to the "Little Mommy" of my dreams and to each one of our mothers and fathers. Your continuing zest for life and your indomitable spirits are an inspiration for all of us.

Acknowledgments

To Jill Crossland, my dedicated editor and business coach: Thank you for your unflagging commitment to making this book the best it can possibly be, for teaching me so much about writing in a way that speaks to my readers, and for your continuing belief in my ability to rise to all the new challenges in my life.

Many thanks to Terri Pepin, my talented and patient 'web angel' who, despite all odds, designed and formatted this book for me. Your creative ideas have added an extra dimension to this book.

Thank you to all of you who read and gave me your valuable input on sections of my book: Diane, Don, Bronwen, Rose, Jan, Kathy M., Vera, Judith, Shawn, Keith, and Susan.

Special thanks to Kathy V. and David for your excellent input and copyright help, and to Martha for copyright information and for your continuing generosity.

Thank you to Don and Bronwen for your unfailing support of me in every way during our life together.

To the many people who make up my network of friends and colleagues, I thank you for believing in me and encouraging me in my writing.

Finally, I am very appreciative of the ideas and inspiration I have drawn from the work and philosophies of Martha Beck, Byron Katie and Judith Duerk.

NOTES:

About the Author

Ellen Besso holds a Master of Arts degree in Counseling Psychology; she is a Martha Beck Certified Coach and a Registered Clinical Counselor. As a writer and life coach she helps midlife women bring balance into their life.

Ellen is also the caregiver for her elderly mother who has Alzheimer's. They always enjoy their weekly outings together and her mom, Glenys, loves to get out and see people.

In writing Surviving Eldercare: Where Their Needs End and Yours Begin, Ellen has brought together her expertise as coach and counselor as well as her own experiences as a midlife caregiver. This book is written for every woman caring for an aging parent or relative with its focus on the person behind the role. It will bring clarity to the emotions and thoughts, awareness of the physical, mental and spiritual needs; as well as examining the dynamics behind the changing parent-daughter relationship and feelings of guilt and loneliness. Ellen shows midlife caregivers how to take care of themselves and ultimately thrive while in this challenging role.

Ellen recently returned from a trip to Southeast Asia where she visited with her brother, who spends his winters on a small, idyllic island in the south of Thailand; she also took some time to go hiking in Laos. In the autumn of 2009 Ellen will make her second visit to India where she will realize her dream of doing volunteer work in Dharamsala, teaching English to Tibetan refugees.

Ellen lives with her partner, Don on the Sunshine Coast of British Columbia, a place she calls her spiritual home. She stays connected and rejuvenated through the study of Buddhist teachings, her Pure Motion dance-exercise classes and visits with her 29 year old daughter, Bronwen. Time spent walking or in her garden with its beautiful roses and coniferous trees allows her to calm her mind.

To contact Ellen Besso:
Email: ellen@ellenbesso.com
Call: 800 961 1364 or 604 886 1916
Website: http://www.ellenbesso.com